BluePrint
Bible Lessons
for Kids

BluePrint Bible Lessons for Kids

52 Lessons
for Preschool through Grade 5

Pam McLagan

Halo ••••
Publishing International

Unless otherwise noted, all Scriptures are taken from the *Holy Bible, New International Version*, *NIV*. Copyright © 1973, 1978, 1984 by Biblica, Inc.™ Used by permission of Zondervan. All rights reserved worldwide. www.zondervan.com

Scripture references marked KJV are taken from the *King James Version* of the Bible.

Scripture references marked ESV are taken from *The Holy Bible: English Standard Version*, copyright © 2001, Wheaton: Good News Publishers. Used by permission. All rights reserved.

Scripture references marked GNT are taken from the *Good News Translation* (Today's English Version, Second Edition) Copyright © 1992 American Bible Society. All rights reserved. This translation is known as the Good News Bible (GNB) around the world.

ISBN: 978-1-61244-268-6
Library of Congress Control Number: 2014908934

Printed in the United States of America

Halo ●●●● Published by Halo Publishing International
Publishing International AP# 726
P.O. Box 60326
Houston, Texas 77205
Toll Free 1-877-705-9647
Website: www.halopublishing.com
E-mail: contact@halopublishing.com

Thanks to teachers at Grace Christian Fellowship (now Grace City Church) for whom this was originally written. Thanks to preschool directors and children's ministry coordinators on both coasts who used this curriculum and added their expertise.
And special thanks to Bill who encouraged me to do this!

Contents

THE LESSONS

FALL QUARTER

God Creates the World

WINTER QUARTER

Advent: The Promised Savior Is Born; God Honors Those Who Obey

Welcome to BluePrint Lessons for Kids

THIS BOOK GREW out of a need for teacher creativity. I was coordinating children's classes at our church and co-teaching a precocious group of four- and five-year-olds. Most of these children had been "born in the pew" and had a good mastery of basic Bible stories. They were bored with simplified material that took six weeks to teach creation. And even though our lesson time was only during the sermon, we usually had about an hour in the classroom. Our solution was to step up the curriculum a bit. What you hold is a result of that effort. We often taught the story directly from a modern translation Bible. We taught about the Trinity. We spent many weeks on a memory portion, which might include several verses. And mothers who thought their preschoolers could "never" learn The Lord's Prayer were astonished to find that not only could the children learn longer passages of Scripture, they were delighted to do it.

Since then, these lessons have been used in church programs with children between the ages of three and ten. They have been used in preschools. Teachers have included teens who like kids; public school teachers in training; moms and dads; experienced pre-school teachers; and Mr. George, storyteller extraordinaire.

What you will find is a BluePrint – not a script.

First will be the Scripture portion that includes the story. Teachers and helpers should be familiar with the biblical portion so they can accurately recount it to the children.

Second will be the memory section. This passage will usually be connected to three or four lessons. That gives plenty of time for the children to learn it and learn it well.

Next is a "Consider" section for teachers and helpers. This segment is to comment, give outside information, or just provide a different outlook on something the teacher is already familiar with.

Fourth is a section called "Our Children" and attempts to bring the lesson into sync with the children. You know your group best and can certainly adapt to the age spans and maturity levels you deal with.

The next section deals with new words and terms that the children may not know. It's amazing how much even preschoolers can learn when we let them. So don't "dumb" things down! Preschoolers know what a "promise" is, and they can learn what a "covenant" is.

Last, you'll find suggestions for "something to make or do." Or you can use your imagination. In addition, many organizations have material online which is available at no cost. All you have to do is click and print. Have fun adapting to suit the children in your care.

Teaching with Style

THIS IS HOW teachers take the WHAT to the WHOM.

No matter how long we've been teaching, we can always use an update or a boost to our styles.

We have been created to learn in four different ways: visual, auditory, kinesthetic, and tactile – see, hear, do, and touch. So think about how God teaches us.

He teaches visually. Remember the rainbow after the flood in Noah's day: a big, bright overhead! This teaching tool is not only big and bright, but also recurring. Other visuals include Jacob's dream of the ladder reaching to heaven; Moses's burning bush; Peter's vision of the "unclean" animals; the Christmas star. God gave us eyesight, and He uses visuals to help us remember the lessons He is teaching us.

So how can we use visuals to help our children learn? How about coloring pictures? Or crossword puzzles? The wordless book? Does your church or organization have a felt board or "flannel graph" hiding in a closet somewhere? Our twenty-first century children are used to videos and flashing pictures, but sometimes, it's not bad to let them just look at something that's NOT moving.

Depending on the age of the children, teachers might use a globe to show where countries are or to illustrate creation. A poster hung in the classroom could remind the children of a lesson or a memory verse. Children could also create their own visuals with a mural of a series of stories.

We can help our children by teaching them to use their eyes!

Teaching with Style – Auditory

In our culture, we are used to multi-sensory learning. Few of us are truly auditory learners; that is, we are not really trained to use our ears! However, it's another port for learning.

God teaches us through sound. Think of the Passover: crackling fires, roasting meat dripping juices that sizzled on the fire, weeping and wailing as the angel of death passed through the nation of Egypt. Or what about Elijah's wind, earthquake, fire, and still small voice? Can we forget the roar of the crowd singing "Hosanna!" when Jesus rode into Jerusalem? Or some of those same voices shouting "crucify Him!" a few days later?

While we probably wouldn't use the auditory alone, it can be a powerful way to learn.

Often we think that children cannot understand "technical" or biblical words, so we attempt to use the simplest words we can. That works to a point. However, children can learn bigger words; they can use their ears.

One day, I was driving through our valley with my two sons. The baby was asleep in the back seat, so the two-year-old and I were having a conversation about what we were seeing. Many interesting crops are grown here, and some need watering during our relatively dry summers. We passed a field of beans that was being irrigated, so I took the opportunity to teach my son a new word. "See the water, Son. They are irrigating the field. When farmers water the crops, it's called irrigation." Soon he was spotting irrigation all over the place, and it was very fun to hear him say "ir-ri-GAY-shun."

The children in our Bible classes can learn biblical words, too. Of course, some will catch on sooner than others depending on their ages and their personal affinity to words, but we should always take the opportunities we have to call them into maturity.

Messiah, Gospel, dedicate, and temple are some of the words the children might be exposed to. We could always use "promised one" instead of Messiah, but then they would lose out on a wonderful word that is used in many ways in our society. "Dedicate" is another word that is used in many situations: train stations are dedicated, buildings, people, children. What a great word to know when one is three.

Teaching with Style – Kinesthetic

Kinesthetic learners absorb information through movement. The information is glued to them as they move. How do we learn to play a musical instrument or learn to write? We play the notes or chords over and over until our fingers and hands know the pattern so well we can do it in our sleep. How do we learn to ski? Or learn to sing a song? We do it over and over again. Our bodies or our mouths and tongues learn the patterns.

God teaches us through movement, too. The people of Israel marched around Jericho. They built altars of stones. They sacrificed animals. Naaman had to wash in the Jordan River seven times. Jesus broke bread; He walked on water; He touched blind eyes; He washed dirty feet.

How do we teach children through movement? Children love songs that have action! Make up movements to songs, clap, wave your arms. Have children who are able write out their memory verses. Put the words of a verse on individual note cards and have the children arrange them in order. Write out the names of the books of the Bible on cards and have the kids put them in order on the floor. If someone knows American Sign Language, have him or her teach the children the signs for a song they love (or find one on YouTube!).

Children love to play-act. Have them act out the story.

Movement helps get wiggles out of little ones, and it helps them learn!

Teaching with Style – Tactile

Touch. God has made us so that we cannot live without the touch of others. Babies who are not held, cradled, rocked, and soothed by the hand of another die or grow up marred. God teaches us with touch and wants us to touch others also.

We often talk about how God "touches" us. Sometimes, we mean it in a figurative sense, but He does teach us with touch. Go back again to the Passover. Think back before the crackling fire and sizzling juices. Think of the wooly lambs, the sticky blood, the rough doorposts. What was God teaching the people with these tactile things? Think of the oil being poured over the head of the high priest. Think of the squishy sand as the Israelites walked through the Red Sea and the Jordan River. Think of the disciples plucking off the heads of grain and rubbing them in their hands. Think of Jesus touching the blind man so he could see; think of Jesus washing the disciples' rough, dirty, calloused feet; think of Him laying His hands on the heads of the children to bless them. Touch.

One teacher brought a candle to class so the children could feel the heat of the "fire" used for sacrifice. Little children can make "sheep" with cotton balls. Have the children break the unleavened Matzoh crackers for communion or Seder … they have a satisfying "crack" to them.

Putting It All Together

Now let's put it all together: visual, auditory, kinesthetic, tactile.

Psalm 119:11 says, "I have hidden your word in my heart that I might not sin against you."

When we have the Word of God in our minds and hearts, He can remind us in times of temptation and stress. It is important to get the Word into the children NOW. Do they understand all of it? NO. Does it matter? NO. Get it in, and God can illuminate it in their lives when they need it.

When our children were preschoolers, we sang Scripture songs in church all the time. We had tapes of Scripture songs; we sang them in the car; we made them up so the boys could learn their Sunday school verses each week. One day, my three-year-old son was outside in the carport dancing and singing,

For I am persuaded, that neither death, nor life, nor angels, nor principalities, nor powers, nor things present, nor things to come, nor height, nor depth, nor any other creature, shall be able to separate us from the love of God, which is in Christ Jesus our Lord.

—Romans 8:38–39 (KJV)

Did he understand all of that at three? No. However, he grew up, went to college, and became an Air Force officer. One night during his training to be a navigator on a tanker plane, things were not going well, and he was getting nervous. Suddenly, he felt hands on his shoulders and the assurance that all was okay. No human person put hands on his shoulders. Was he learning and remembering something about the love of God just then? Yes! Because it was in him, God could remind him.

It is important that teachers work on the memory verse each week. How to do that?

Visual: Write it out. Children who can write, can copy the verse…. They see it, say it, do it, touch it. Those who can't yet read could draw pictures around the verse that teachers have printed on paper.

Auditory/Kinesthetic – say it/hear it: Repeat the verse several times. Learn phrases at a time. Don't try to do the whole thing at once, and don't go word-by-word. It needs to make sense.

"I have hidden your word in my heart"
… [repeat several times]
"that I might not sin against you."
[repeat several times]

Put it together:
"I have hidden your word in my heart that I might not sin against you." [repeat several times]
Psalm 119:11 [Repeat several times]

Put It Together

"I have hidden your word in my heart that I might not sin against you." Psalm 119:11

Kinesthetic/Tactile: Add rhythm, make up a tune, add motions.

And there you have it! Teaching with all ports!

The Lessons

Fall Quarter

Memory work for the quarter:

Weeks 1–3 – Genesis 1:1 "In the beginning God created the heavens and the earth." (NIV)

Weeks 4–6 – Isaiah 43:1 "Fear not, for I have redeemed you; I have called you by name; you are mine." (ESV)

Weeks 7–10 – Jeremiah 29:11 "'For I know the plans I have for you,' declares the Lord, 'plans to prosper you and not to harm you, plans to give you hope and a future.'" (NIV)

Weeks 11–13 – Psalm 92:1–2 "It is a good thing to give thanks unto the Lord and to sing praises unto Thy name, O Most High, to show forth Thy lovingkindness in the morning and Thy faithfulness every night." (KJV)

Welcome to the first quarter of these BluePrint Lessons for kids.

In these lessons, we go to the beginning when God created the heavens and the earth. For decades, people have been debating the merits of evolution (the facts, as they say) and creation (myth, as they say). Actually, we must take both ideas on faith. Hebrews 11:3 says that "By faith we understand that the universe was formed at God's command, so that what is seen was not made out of what was visible." Evolutionists, too, must take their beliefs by faith simply because no one living now was there to witness the beginning. Creation by God is not "scientifically provable" in the sense that doubters want proof. (But then, neither is evolution! It's not repeatable!!)

Our themes for the quarter are God Creates the World and God Chooses a People. God created the world for a general revelation of Himself, and God chose a people through whom to reveal Himself specifically through law and grace.

Covenants (a binding and solemn agreement to keep or do a certain thing) figure strongly in this series of lessons. The first covenant is with all people of the earth given to Noah after the flood. Then God makes promises to Abraham, Isaac, and Jacob. It's important for children to be exposed to these covenants. They then can begin to add the promises of God and the fulfillments of those promises into their memory banks so they, too, can build faith.

The last lessons of the quarter deal with giving thanks.

Have a great time with these foundational truths!

God Creates the World

Scripture: Genesis 1–2:4

Memory Verse: "In the beginning, God created the heavens and the earth." Genesis 1:1

Consider: "Let there be …; and there was …." God spoke it into being. The world that God spoke into being is not the world as we know it. The original earth had a water canopy, which protected the inhabitants from the ultraviolet rays of the sun. The weather was likely tropical in nature – all over the world. Twenty-first century people are no different from others.

Ancient people had many explanations for the creation they saw all around them. They saw the powerful seas and reasoned that there must be a god – some very powerful being – who controlled that sea. They saw lightning and decided it must be an angry god tossing the "bolts." Each group of people had its own way of explaining how the earth came about. The Bible teaches that an all-powerful God spoke the world into existence.

Many Bible students are concerned with the six days of creation: were these six twenty-four-hour days or longer periods of time? Even now we use the word "day" in many ways just as the ancient Hebrews did. We speak of a "day of reckoning," "days of opportunity," or even "days of silence." These may mean literal twenty-four-hour days or just a period of time. Biblical writers speak of a "day of the Lord," a "day of judgment," and a "day of God's wrath."

Actually, none of that makes any difference:

By faith we understand that the world was framed by the word of God, so that the things which are seen were not made of things which are visible.
—Hebrews 11:3

Our Children do not need to be embroiled in the creation controversy. We do not need to explain the length of a "day." What they need to know at this point is that a loving, powerful, just God created everything – including them! With that thought firmly in place, they can weather the controversies that will come later. They will have confidence that no matter how God did it, they are special, not an accident or a mutant. They have special responsibilities, just as Adam and Eve had, and special privileges: Because of Jesus, they can go into the "holy of holies."

New words to learn or review:

1. Create: To cause to come into existence. When we talk of creation, we refer here to the bringing into being of the physical universe.

Something to Make or Do:

Have children draw the days of creation and create a "time line" for the room. These can be done on individual sheets of paper (Day 1, Day 2, etc.) or on a piece of "butcher paper."

God Creates People in His Own Image, The Trinity

Scripture: Genesis 1:26 to 2:24

Memory Verse: "In the beginning, God created the heavens and the earth." Genesis 1:1 (NIV)

Consider Genesis 1:26–27. "Then God said, 'Let us make man in our image, in our likeness, and let them rule over the fish of the sea and the birds of the air, over the livestock, over all the earth, and over all the creatures that move along the ground.' So God created man in his own image, in the image of God he created him; male and female he created them." (NIV)

Just what is "the image of God?"

Obviously, we are not perfect or all-powerful or all-knowing. Perhaps it is our three-part-ness: body, soul, spirit. Our bodies are the physical, visible parts; our souls – mind, will, and emotions – are not visible; and our spirits – the parts of us that communicate with God – are also not visible. God, too, is triune: Father, Son, and Holy Spirit. Each one points to the other and communicates with the other. God is ONE as He expressed himself to Israel, but Jesus clearly taught of the Trinity. And that was not unusual for the Hebrews; that was not what they killed Jesus for.

In Genesis, we see the Trinity working together to create people. "Let us make man in our image, in our likeness; male and female he created them" (Genesis 1:26–27 NIV).

While we refer to God as male, it took male and female people to fully represent the "likeness of God." Adam was not complete in himself. Women were not an after-thought.

Our Children can begin to get an idea of the Trinity, the triune nature of God. Of course, it is a complex idea. Most adults have difficulty understanding it. But children are able, through their eyes of faith, to grasp bigger concepts than many of us are willing to admit.

Teaching tip: Bring to class several items which have three parts, and yet are one: egg (shell, white, yolk); squash (skin, meat, seeds); apricots, peaches, pears (skin, meat, seeds); a clover or shamrock (three leaves). To help the children understand their own three-part-ness, we can talk about their bodies, souls (mind, will, and emotions), and spirits (that part that communicates with God).

Words to learn or review:

1. Create: To cause to come into existence. When we talk of creation, we refer here to the beginning of the physical universe.
2. Trinity: The concept of one God Who exists in three distinct personalities, perfect in love and harmony with each other.

Something to Make or Do:

1. Make or draw a clover or shamrock to help the children understand the concept of "three in one."
2. Or you might use water in its three states: liquid, ice, steam. They are different looking but all the same substance. Or have the children think of a word. Then the thought is compared to the Father. Speaking the word is compared to the Son ("In the beginning was the Word" John 1:1). And the breath you feel when you speak into your hand is the Spirit.

Adam and Eve Disobey God

Scripture: Genesis 3

Memory Verse: "In the beginning, God created the heavens and the earth." Genesis 1:1 (NIV)

Consider: When God put Adam and Eve in the garden, He told them, "You are free to eat from any tree in the garden; but you must not eat from the tree of the knowledge of good and evil, for when you eat of it you will surely die." Yet when Eve talked to the serpent (isn't it interesting that Eve was not astonished the serpent was talking to her!) she said God told them not even to touch the tree! It seems that human beings have always wanted to expand on God's laws.

Adam and Eve decided to disobey God and eat of the fruit of the tree of the knowledge of good and evil, and when they did, "the eyes of both of them were opened, and they realized they were naked, so they sewed fig leaves together and made coverings for themselves" (Genesis 3:7). Then they went to hide from God.

Then God confronted the pair and asked them three questions:

1. Where are you? (Why are you hiding?)
2. Who told you that you were naked? (Why did you believe someone else?)
3. What have you done? (Are you ready to take responsibility for it?)

In typical human fashion, Adam and Eve pass the buck: It was someone else's fault. Adam passed the buck to Eve and Eve passed it to the serpent. So God started with the serpent: "Cursed are you … And I will put hostility between you and the woman and between your offspring and hers; he will crush your head, and you will strike his heel." And thus, God gave the first prophecy concerning a savior! Then God turned to Eve and told her that she would have pain in childbirth and that her husband would rule over her. Then on to Adam: "Cursed is the ground because of you…."

Next, God made clothing of skins for them, no doubt introducing the concept of sacrifice.

Indeed, the day they ate of the tree of the knowledge of good and evil, death came to the earth for the first time.

Our Children can understand the concept of deliberate disobedience. Mom and Dad say, "Do not …" and they do it anyway. God clearly showed in Genesis 3 that there must be consequences to disobedience. When Adam and Eve sinned, they broke fellowship with God. God did not love them less, but He had to send them out of the garden so they would not eat of the tree of life and live forever in sin! When our children disobey, they reap consequences, too. They break fellowship with Mom and Dad and need to mend it by repentance and renewed obedience. God showed Adam and Eve how to renew their fellowship. We show the children how to renew their fellowship with God and with whomever they have disobeyed.

Something to Make or Do:

1. Act out the story.
2. Act out obeying Mom and Dad. Perhaps you can show how obeying is much quicker than whining!

Noah and the Ark

Scripture: Genesis 5–9

Memory Verse: "Fear not, for I have redeemed you; I have called you by name; you are mine." Isaiah 43:1 (ESV)

Consider: If we count the years and generations of humans on the earth, we find that in not many generations, the world was so corrupt that God was "grieved that he had made man on the earth." (Genesis 6:6). People have always followed their own sinful inclinations. But as in the case of Noah, and later, Lot, God preserved someone who would obey Him and follow His commandments.

"Noah found favor in the eyes of the Lord…. Noah was a righteous man, blameless among the people of his time, and he walked with God" (Genesis 6:8–9). And Shem, Ham, and Japheth were born after he was 500 years old! (Genesis 5:32).

God gave Noah some very specific instructions about how to build the vessel that would save the Noah family and all the animals that would be preserved. If you have time before you teach this lesson, view one of the videos about the ark. Like everything else that is of the miraculous, we must take the ark story on faith. But there are people living who have seen the ark on Mt. Ararat, geology shows evidence of a world-wide flood, and simulations have shown that it would be possible for such a vessel to be built and that it would, indeed, do the job.

Our Children have, no doubt, already heard this story. So let's go deeper with them this time. Read directly from a modern language Bible, rather than from a storybook. The children are usually shocked to learn that Noah was to take seven (or seven pairs) of every kind of clean animal. That does not make what they have learned before wrong, it just means

that now they are growing up and can understand more of what God has said in His Word.

We can look at this lesson in several ways:

1. God preserved and cared for Noah and his family, and He will care for us.
2. Noah was obedient and thankful. He obeyed God in the building of the ark, and he thanked God with a *real* sacrifice when they came out.
3. There are grave consequences to sin. It pains God. And in this case, He destroyed the known world. But He also created a covenant between Himself, Noah's family, and "for all generations to come" that He would not destroy all life with a flood again!

New words to learn or review:

1. Ark – as used here, a large vessel (boat) used to house Noah, his family, and all the animals.
2. Covenant – a binding and solemn agreement to keep or do a certain thing. In this case, it is God's covenant with Noah and for all generations to come that He would not destroy all life with a flood again!

Something to Make or Do:

1. A contractor in the Netherlands has built a scale model of the ark for people to visit. An Internet search for "Noah's Ark Replica Holland" should guide you to the site with photos of the scale model of the ark.
2. Act out the story. Bring some soft toys to be the animals, or have the children pretend to be lions, zebras, or cats!
3. Have each child draw a piece of the story and then take turns telling his or her part.

The Tower of Babel

Scripture: Genesis 11:1–9

Memory Verse: "Fear not, for I have redeemed you; I have called you by name; you are mine." Isaiah 43:1 (NIV)

Consider: Here they are again. God had destroyed the whole world because of the sinfulness of people, and within a few generations again, they were planning how to build a tower to the heavens and become famous. The other part of the plan was not to be scattered. This, of course, was a direct violation of God's Word to the people after the flood. They were to populate the earth, but they wanted to stay together on that wonder plain in Shinar.

So God fixed them! The Trinity came down and confused their languages. If they could not understand each other, then they would be stifled in their attempts at greatness.

Think how frustrating it feels when you hear people speaking a language you do not understand! Or let's say you know a little of a language – "Good morning. Where is the bathroom?" – but you want to communicate something else, something important. You have to work at understanding. You have to work hard to be able to communicate. Most of us don't really try very hard. And we stay separated from our fellow human beings.

Interestingly, it was at Pentecost that God broke down the language barrier.

Now there were staying in Jerusalem God-fearing Jews from every nation under heaven. When they heard this sound, a crowd came together in bewilderment, because each one heard them speaking in his own language.

—Acts 2:5–6

Our Children will find this story interesting. They often want to know how things came to be. It might be fun to learn a greeting or a short verse or song in another language. If you have a recording of children's songs in another language, it would be interesting to listen to those.

God had a reason for confusing the languages. But He also has a reason for us to learn other languages: to tell the good news!

New words to learn or review:

1. Babel – the name of the tower the people wanted to build to reach heaven. It sounds like the Hebrew word for confused.

Something to Make or Do:

1. Learn a song in another language.
2. Create a card with the greeting "Jesus loves you" in other languages. (Check an online translation program for other languages. Many of these include pronunciation.)

Spanish: Jesús te ama.
French: Jésus vous aime.
Indonesian: Yesus mengasihi Anda

God Calls Abram

Scripture: Genesis 12

Memory Verse: "Fear not, for I have redeemed you; I have called you by name; you are mine." Isaiah 43:1 (ESV)

Consider: Abram moved from Ur of the Chaldeans with his father and family to the place they called Haran. When Abram was seventy-five years old, God spoke to him:

> Leave your country, your people and your father's household and go to the land I will show you. I will make you into a great nation and I will bless you; I will make your name great, and you will be a blessing. I will bless those who bless you, and whoever curses you I will curse; and all peoples on earth will be blessed through you.
>
> —Genesis 12:1–3

Why did God choose this man to be the one through whom He would redeem the world? Perhaps in Abram God found someone who would have faith, who would believe, who would act. Abram (a high father) would later become Abraham (father of nations). Let's remember that the promise was given to a seventy-five-year-old man who had no children and whose wife was considered barren and could not have any children.

Hebrews tells us that "by faith … Abraham …" obeyed and went…. He made his home in the promised land like a stranger … he lived in tents … he was looking forward to the city with foundations whose architect and builder is God. By faith … Abraham was enabled to become a father because he considered him faithful who had made the promise" (Hebrews 11:8–11).

Our Children are capable of great faith also. We all live our lives on faith – faith the car will run, the electricity will work, the boss will pay our wages. Children even more so because they don't have a lot of experience to back them up. So they believe. Adults have disappointments and heartaches, which sometimes prevent us from believing God. Has God let us down? No. But we often have a hard time believing that He will do what He has said. "Lord, I believe; help my unbelief!" (Mark 9:24).

New words to learn or review:

1. Covenant – a binding and solemn agreement to keep or do a certain thing. Here the promise is to Abraham and his family.

Something to Make or Do:

1. Act out the story. Think about what Abram and Sarai would have to do to get ready for such a trip: pack food, make sure tents are in order, gather other provisions.

God Gives Isaac/God Asks Abraham to Sacrifice Isaac

Scripture: Genesis 21–22

Memory Verse: "'For I know the plans I have for you,' declares the Lord, 'plans to prosper you and not to harm you, plans to give you hope and a future.'" Jeremiah 29:11

Teaching tip: Since some of the younger children might not be familiar with the story of the birth of Isaac, review that before you do the story of the sacrifice.

Consider: You waited twenty-five years for this child. You were 100 years old when he was born. God told you this child was "the child of the promise," the one through whom all the nations would be blessed. Then God comes along and tells you that you are to take this child to the mountain and that you are to sacrifice him! What is God doing?

But Genesis tells us that "[e]arly the next morning Abraham got up and saddled his donkey. He took with him two of his servants and his son Isaac. When he had cut enough wood for the burnt offering, he set out for the place God had told him about" (Genesis 22:3). Abraham did not waste any time. He did not argue with God. He just gathered what he needed and set out.

In the end, God did not require the sacrifice of Isaac, but Abraham was ready to obey. Down through history, however, others have been required to sacrifice their children. The Nazis, in the last century, held families hostage and required fathers to deny their faith and their God or their children would be killed. Some fathers did not have the faith of Abraham, but some did. Even today, our children can be "held hostage." They might not be killed, nor are we asked to kill them, but we might be asked to deny our Lord and our faith so they would not be persecuted at school. Can we stand firm?

Our Children might find this story troubling. A father being asked to sacrifice his son? God did not ask His people to sacrifice their children as was the custom in other cultures of the time. What was God doing? It is helpful to remember that Isaac was not a preschooler at this time. He was likely a young teen. He was probably strong, and his father was over 100 years old! Isaac probably could have easily overwhelmed his father and refused to be the sacrifice! But he didn't. He was obedient. He trusted his father, who trusted in God.

New words to learn:

1. Future – what is coming, a time yet to come
2. Hope – the desire for something that a person believes can be obtained or expects he will get.

Something to Make or Do:

1. Think of ways God provides for us: food, shelter, clothing, friends. Draw these or make a collage to show God's provision.

God Provides a Wife for Isaac

Scripture: Genesis 24

Memory Verse: "'For I know the plans I have for you,' declares the Lord, 'plans to prosper you and not to harm you, plans to give you hope and a future.'" Jeremiah 29:11 (NIV)

Consider: This is one of those stories where everything goes right. The servant makes the promise to Abraham that he will attempt to get a wife for Isaac from among Abraham's relatives. The servant prays a very specific prayer, and the Lord answers it immediately in the positive. Everything falls into place. The servant takes Rebekah off to Isaac, and he loves her immediately!

When I was a child and heard this story, I remember getting one of those "WOW" feelings. And it is a WOW story. God was doing something wonderful for Abraham, the servant, Isaac, and Rebekah. Abraham wanted to be sure that Isaac had a wife from God-fearing people and not from the idolatrous Canaanites. And when the servant told his story to Rebekah's family, they, too, saw the hand of God in it and agreed to let Rebekah go to Isaac. But they were not unfeeling toward the young woman. When the servant wanted to leave immediately, the family balked. They wanted to wait for ten days – a reasonable request since they had only met the man the night before and Rebekah needed to prepare to go with him. So they asked Rebekah. It was *her* decision. And she opted to go.

Not all stories are as straightforward as this one, but it is an excellent example of what can happen when all of God's people are willing to do things His way.

Our Children are a long way from being marriageable age, but it is not too early for them to realize that marriage is one of those things they need to pray about, as the servant did, and to have God's confirmation in.

Something to Make or Do:

1. Act out the story

Jacob Steals the Birthright and the Blessing

Scripture: Genesis 25:19–34 and Genesis 27:1–46

Memory Verse: "'For I know the plans I have for you,' declares the Lord, 'plans to prosper you and not to harm you, plans to give you hope and a future.'" Jeremiah 29:11 (NIV)

Consider: Jacob and Esau were twins. But twins were never so different. Esau was a man's man. He loved to hunt and was described as "a man of the open country." Jacob was more of a homebody. Men with different missions in life, different interests. Unfortunately, the parents had favorites! Isaac favored Esau, and Rebekah favored Jacob.

In ancient times, the "birthright" was a privilege generally belonging to the firstborn son. In Israel, as in other places, this was a favored position in the family. It included a double portion of the father's assets upon his death and subsequent family leadership responsibilities. The firstborn was also to receive a special blessing.

Since Esau was the first twin born, he held the right to that special place, but Esau sold his birthright for a bowl of stew (Gen. 25:29–34), and Scripture says that he "despised" that privilege and responsibility. The holder of the birthright was to act as priest for the family and lead them in the worship of God, but Esau did not have the faith or inclination to see that as of any value. So that high honor went to Jacob instead.

Our Children: This concept of birthright is foreign to our children, but they can understand the concepts of privilege and responsibility. One has certain responsibilities, so one gets certain privileges. Sometimes these are connected to age. In ancient times, the eldest son had great privileges but also great responsibilities. Esau did not value his privileges and sold them very cheaply. And then Jacob figured out how to get the blessing, too! Is it any wonder that when Esau finally understood the value of the birthright and blessing he was angry enough to kill his brother? Our children can also understand being angry at apparent or real injustices. They and we need to learn to go on by God's grace.

Something to Make or Do:

1. Snack: Lentil soup and bread

Jacob's Dream at Bethel

Scripture: Genesis 28:10–22

Memory Verse: "'For I know the plans I have for you,' declares the Lord, "plans to prosper you and not to harm you, plans to give you hope and a future.'" Jeremiah 29:11 (NIV)

Consider: Jacob tricked his brother out of the birthright, those privileges and responsibilities of the eldest son. Then he tricked his father out of the blessing that should have gone to his brother. Both men knew the value of the blessing, and each one wanted it. But Jacob had Mom working with him to trick Dad. Oh, what a family!

Amazingly, God uses people like Isaac, Jacob, and us to complete what He wants done on the earth. And He communicates to us His promises and plans. Just so, He communicated to Jacob. God spoke to Rebekah about the twins even before their birth and said that the "older will serve the younger." Now Jacob must flee for his life after his plotting and trickery.

But on his first night out on his way to Haran, God spoke to Jacob in the wonderful, famous dream. Genesis 28:13–15:

> There above it (the staircase leading to heaven) stood the LORD, and he said: "I am the LORD, the God of your father Abraham and the God of Isaac. I will give you and your descendants the land on which you are lying. Your descendants will be like the dust of the earth, and you will spread out to the west and to the east, to the north and to the south. All peoples on earth will be blessed through you and your offspring. I am with you and will watch over you wherever you go, and I will bring you back to this land. I will not leave you until I have done what I have promised you. (NIV)

This, of course, echoes what God told Abraham and Isaac. And there seems to be an added promise of God's presence and "watching over" that is not seen in the earlier covenants.

Our Children: Here we have a great opportunity to review the covenant that God made with Abraham (Genesis 12:2–3, 15:18, 22; 15–18) and with Isaac (Genesis 26:24). God again is speaking – this time to the grandson of Abraham and declaring His intent to bless all peoples of the earth through this family. And who is that blessing? Jesus, of course. God keeps His promises!

New words to learn or review:

1. Covenant: a binding and solemn agreement to keep or do a certain thing.

Something to Make or Do:

1. Bring a large smooth stone for the children to use as a "pillow" and act out the story.

Jacob and Esau Are Reconciled

Scripture: Genesis 32–33

Memory Verse: "It is a good thing to give thanks unto the LORD, and to sing praises unto thy name, O Most High: To shew forth thy lovingkindness in the morning, and thy faithfulness every night." Psalm 92:1 (KJV)

Consider: It had been twenty years since Jacob tricked the blessing out of his father. This same father who was supposedly dying and needed to bless his son quickly was still alive! Jacob had met his match in his father-in-law, Laban, and had been tricked in the matter of wives and wages. Now it was time to go back home.

The Lord had prospered Jacob and directed him to return to Canaan and to his family. Jacob, however, was not sure of his welcome with his brother and sent messengers ahead to "test the waters." The messengers came back with the news that Esau was coming with 400 men! An army! And Jacob was coming with wives, children, flocks, and herds! Jacob was afraid. Genesis 32:7 says Jacob was in "fear and distress." Twenty years earlier, Esau wanted to kill him. Had he calmed down? Was Esau still angry? Jacob didn't know. He did know he was supposed to return home and that God would prosper him there. So he sent messengers and gifts to his brother. He gave his servants instructions about how to proceed, sent everyone ahead, and was alone for the night.

During that night "a man wrestled with him until daybreak." Whoever this "man" was, he had supernatural powers. He "touched" Jacob's hip so that it was wrenched. And then the "man" gave Jacob a new name – Israel. He was no longer the trickster, the supplanter, the one who took another's place. He was the one who struggled with God.

The two brothers were reconciled. Esau had done some growing up; God had worked with him, too. They forgave each other, and they eventually buried their father together. God can bring good out of bad situations if we are willing to grow and forgive.

When Jacob got "settled in" at his new home near Shechem, he set up an altar and named it El Elohe Israel (Mighty is the God of Israel). [Interesting, God is no longer the God of my father, but the God of Israel – ME.]

Note: You might want to make note of this altar. Altars generally were set up for giving thanks to God and worshiping God. As the next lessons deal with giving thanks, you might want to mention how Jacob gave thanks to God.

Our Children know what it is like to be angry with a sibling or friend. The world isn't as bright, and they are sad and maybe afraid. But when each admits his or her wrong and is willing to "give" a little, God can bless them and us. See Matthew 5:23–24 and Matthew 18:15–20 for biblical guidance on seeking forgiveness and reconciliation.

New words to learn or review:

1. Forgiveness: The act of letting go of or pardoning another in spite of his slights, shortcomings, and errors. As a theological term, forgiveness refers to God's pardon of the sins of human beings.

Something to Make or Do:

1. Practice "forgiveness" by acting out taking something from someone and then returning it and asking forgiveness.

Why Should We Thank God?

Memory Verse: "It is a good thing to give thanks unto the LORD, and to sing praises unto thy name, O Most High: To shew forth thy lovingkindness in the morning, and thy faithfulness every night." Psalm 92:1 (KJV)

Scripture/Consider:

Why should we thank God?

> Give thanks to the LORD, for he is good; his love endures forever.
> —1 Chronicles 16:34, NIV

> I will give thanks to the LORD because of his righteousness and will sing praise to the name of the LORD Most High.
> —Psalm 7:17, NIV

> The LORD is my strength and my shield; my heart trusts in him, and I am helped. My heart leaps for joy and I will give thanks to him in song.
> —Psalm 28:7, NIV

> We give thanks to you, O God, we give thanks, for your Name is near; men tell of your wonderful deeds.
> —Psalm 75:1, NIV

> Give thanks to the LORD, call on his name; make known among the nations what he has done.
> —Psalm 105:1, NIV

> Let them give thanks to the LORD for his unfailing love and his wonderful deeds for men.
> —Psalm 107:8, NIV

> Give thanks to the God of heaven. His love endures forever.
> —Psalm 136:26, NIV

> Give thanks to the LORD Almighty, for the LORD is good; his love endures forever.
> —Jeremiah 33:11, NIV

> It is a good thing to give thanks unto the Lord and to sing praises unto Thy name, O Most High, to show forth Thy lovingkindness in the morning and Thy faithfulness every night.
> —Psalm 92:1, KJV

Giving thanks to the Lord is part of what we need to do as human creatures. This is different from feeling thankful.

Consider: Some thoughts on Psalm 50:14 and 23

> Let the giving of thanks be your sacrifice to God, and give the Almighty all that you promised.
> —Psalm 50:14, GNT

> Giving thanks is the sacrifice that honors me, and I will surely save all who obey me.
> —Psalm 50:23, GNT

These verses first popped off the page for me a number of years ago. We had just been through a winter of asthma for our middle son, and we had just moved to the smog capital of the world, the San Bernardino Valley. I was concerned! (I didn't know then that said son was not particularly allergic to or sensitive to smog, just grass and dust and mites.) Why, Lord, have you brought us here to have our child be sick? Thousands of kids have asthma problems here, etc., etc.

Then God took me to Psalm 50. Okay. A sacrifice of praise, eh?

In the Old Testament, the sacrifices were to be offered for all sorts of things, and they had to be the best or the first – hard to give up. We like to keep the best of what we have; and I suspect the first-fruits of the crops were hard to give up simply because they were the first.

So the sacrifice is that which is due to God, but that which is hard to give up, and which we would like to keep. But I found that as I gave thanks for the place where we were, all those anxieties dropped away. It was a great three years there in Smogsville.

Then the Lord took me backward in the chapter to verse 8 and following: "I do not reprimand you because of your sacrifices and the burnt offerings you always bring me. And yet I do not need bulls from your farms or goats from your flocks; all the animals in the forest are mine and the cattle on thousands of hills. All the wild birds are mine and all living things in the fields."

God does not need the things we bring Him or even our works. He owns all the things. What He wants is our thanks. Notice that it doesn't even say "be thankful." It says, "give thanks." A very subtle difference. When we moved to the San Bernardino area, I did not feel thankful! But I did give thanks. There will be times when the feeling of thankfulness will be far away, but we are to give thanks anyway. Why? Because it is hard to do; because it is valuable; and because it is due to God.

Our Children need to learn to give thanks. Not because they feel like it, but because they should; it is due to God. Review with the children some of the Bible people who gave thanks, praised God, built altars, etc: Noah, Abraham, Isaac, Jacob. And we might review *how* we can thank God.

The priests took their positions, as did the Levites with the LORD's musical instruments, which King David had made for praising the LORD and which were used when he gave thanks … Opposite the Levites, the priests blew their trumpets….

—2 Chronicles 7:6, NIV

The LORD is my strength and my shield; my heart trusts in him, and I am helped. My heart leaps for joy and I will give thanks to him in song.

—Psalm 28:7, NIV

I will give you thanks in the great assembly, among throngs of people I will praise you.

—Psalm 35:18, NIV

Give thanks to the LORD, call on his name; make known among the nations what he has done. Sing to him, sing praise to him; tell of all his wonderful acts.

—1 Chronicles 16:8–9, NIV

Remember the wonders he has done, his miracles, and the judgments he ronounced.

—1 Chronicles 16:12, NIV

Sing to the LORD, all the earth; proclaim his salvation day after day. Declare his glory among the nations, his marvelous deeds among all peoples.

—1 Chronicles 16:23–24, NIV

Ascribe to the LORD the glory due his name. Bring an offering and come before him; worship the LORD in the splendor of his holiness.

—1 Chronicles 16:29, NIV

Something to Make or Do:

1. Learn a song of thanksgiving.
2. Make a placemat with things children are thankful for.

For What Should We Thank God?

Memory Verse: "It is a good thing to give thanks unto the LORD, and to sing praises unto thy name, O Most High: To shew forth thy lovingkindness in the morning, and thy faithfulness every night." Psalm 92:1 (KJV)

Scripture/Consider:

For What Should We Thank God? Ultimately, we give thanks "in everything."

> Let them give thanks to the LORD for his unfailing love and his wonderful deeds for men.
> —Psalm 107:8, NIV

> I will give you thanks, for you answered me; you have become my salvation.
> —Psalm 118:21, NIV

> You are my God, and I will give you thanks; you are my God, and I will exalt you.
> —Psalm 118:28, NIV

> At midnight I rise to give you thanks for your righteous laws.
> —Psalm 119:62, NIV

> And he directed the people to sit down on the grass. Taking the five loaves and the two fish and looking up to heaven, he gave thanks and broke the loaves. Then he gave them to the disciples, and the disciples gave them to the people.
> —Matthew 14:19, NIV

> Coming up to them at that very moment, she gave thanks to God and spoke about the child (Jesus) to all who were looking forward to the redemption of Jerusalem.
> —Luke 2:38, NIV

> But thanks be to God! He gives us the victory through our Lord Jesus Christ.
> —1 Corinthians 15:57, NIV

> But thanks be to God, who always leads us in triumphal procession in Christ and through us spreads everywhere the fragrance of the knowledge of him.
> —2 Corinthians 2:14, NIV

> Thanks be to God for his indescribable gift!
> —2 Corinthians 9:15, NIV

> Always giving thanks to God the Father for everything, in the name of our Lord Jesus Christ.
> —Ephesians 5:20, NIV

> Giving thanks to the Father, who has qualified you to share in the inheritance of the saints in the kingdom of light.
> —Colossians 1:12, NIV

> Give thanks in all circumstances, for this is God's will for you in Christ Jesus.
> —1 Thessalonians 5:18, NIV

> "… We give thanks to you, Lord God Almighty, the One who is and who was, because you have taken your great power and have begun to reign."
> —Revelation 11:17, NIV

Our children can understand that all things come from God, and we should recognize that and thank Him for all things. Review with the children some of the past lessons and what Bible people gave thanks for: children, healings, resurrections, food.

Something to Make or Do:

1. A Thanksgiving placemat. Have the children draw or cut out things for which they are thankful. Use legal-sized paper. When they are finished, you can cover the mats with clear contact paper so the children can use them as placemats.
2. Sing a song of thanksgiving. Use instruments.
3. Make a mural of things to be thankful for.

Winter Quarter

The winter quarter finds us in Advent – looking forward to the birth of the Messiah. The focus will be on the obedience of the people involved. We then move to considering Jesus' growing up, being baptized and tempted, calling the disciples, and teaching leaders and others who want to know. Come along.

Advent: The Promised Savior Is Born; God Honors Those Who Obey

Jesus Grows Up and Begins His Ministry

Memory work for the quarter:

Lessons 1–5: "Jesus said, 'Blessed (rather) are those who hear the word of God and obey it.'"

—Luke 11:28, NIV

Lessons 6–8: "Children, obey your parents in the Lord, for this is right."

—Ephesians 6:1, NIV

Lessons 9–13: "Come, follow me," Jesus said, "and I will make you fishers of men."

—Matthew 4:19, NIV

John the Baptist Is Born

Scripture: Luke 1:5–15 and Luke 1:57–80

Memory Verse: "Jesus said, 'Blessed (rather) are those who hear the word of God and obey it.'" Luke 11:28 (NIV)

Consider: John and Jesus were earthly cousins. John was the son of a priest, Zechariah, and Mary's relative, Elizabeth. Scripture tells us that John was the "voice of one crying in the wilderness" prophesied in Isaiah.

When Gabriel appeared to Zechariah and told him of John's arrival, the old man must have been incredulous! He and his wife were old! How could they have a child? I find it interesting that his words and Mary's words at the angel's announcement are nearly the same (at least in English!), but the angel's response is very different. Evidently Gabriel detected doubt in Zechariah's words and a request for information in Mary's. Zechariah was not able to speak until John was born; Mary got the information she requested. However, Zechariah must have been convinced since he went home and John was conceived!

When the baby was born, Zechariah and Elizabeth obeyed and named him John – even though none of the family had that name. God honored those who obeyed.

Our Children are full of wonder and believing. Help them see a man the age of a grandpa standing before God doing his job. Suddenly, an angel is standing there telling him the fantastic news that he will be a father! Help them see a woman the age of a grandma receiving the news that she will have a baby. And then that wonderful baby arrives. They give him the name of John which means "Jehovah is gracious."

New words to learn:

Gospel is a word that means "good news." We use the word to mean two different things:

1. the story about Jesus coming to earth to save us and
2. one of the first four books of the New Testament (Matthew, Mark, Luke, and John)

The stories this quarter will come from the Gospels. Try to work the word "Gospel" into each week's lesson.

Messiah is a word that means "anointed" and is used to mean Jesus. The Hebrew people waited for the Messiah (as many still do). The Greek word is Christ. The person who is anointed is the king.

Something to Make or Do:

1. Bookmarks to color or paint
2. Christmas cards

The Birth of Jesus Is Announced

Scripture: Luke 1:26–56 and Matthew 1:18–24

Memory Verse: "Jesus said, 'Blessed (rather) are those who hear the word of God and obey it.'" Luke 11:28 (NIV)

Consider: Gabriel had some interesting news for Mary: She would be the mother of the Messiah. As adults, we can imagine the sorts of thoughts that must have raced through Mary's head. *What is this? What about Joseph? What will he say? My family will never believe this! How will this be since I am a virgin?*

Protestants have historically downplayed Mary's role in all this. And yet, she must have been an exemplary young woman who was going to be misunderstood for the rest of her life. She knew, no doubt, that she would be shunned, ridiculed, talked about, and generally scorned. And yet, she said, "I am the Lord's servant. May it be to me as you have said" (Luke 1:38). Mary was obedient.

Joseph, too, was obedient. Matthew 1:19 says that he was a "righteous man." He didn't jump right in and call off the marriage, but "considered" the matter. When the angel came to him in a dream and told him about the baby, he "did what the Lord had commanded." He, too, would be misunderstood. By marrying Mary, he accepted responsibility for the child. I'm sure that in the eyes of the town, he was guilty!

Our Children: There is always the possibility with this story that the children will ask something to the effect, "What's the big deal? Why would being pregnant before marriage be so bad?" After all, this is a part of the world we live in and may be a part of our own family structure. This really isn't the time for sex education, but we can tell the children that God's plan for families is that people be married first. In Bible times, if a woman became pregnant before her wedding day, she and the child suffered. At this point in the children's lives, let's not make a big deal about this. If they ask, try to deal with it in a low-key way and then recommend they talk with their parents about it.

In the meantime, let's focus on Mary and Joseph's obedience.

New words to learn:

Gospel is a word that means "good news." We use the word to mean two different things:

1. the story about Jesus coming to earth to save us and
2. one of the first four books of the New Testament (Matthew, Mark, Luke, and John)

The stories this quarter will come from the Gospels. Work the word "Gospel" into each week's lesson.

Messiah is a word that means "anointed" and is used to mean Jesus. The Hebrew people waited for the Messiah (as many still do). The Greek word is Christ. The person who is anointed is the king.

Something to Make or Do:

1. Act out the story
2. Draw pictures on big paper
3. Bookmarks or Christmas cards
4. Nativity scenes
5. Decorate soup cans for pencil holder gifts

The Journey to Bethlehem

Scripture: Luke 2

Memory Verse: "Jesus said, 'Blessed (rather) are those who hear the word of God and obey it.'" Luke 11:28 (NIV)

Consider: This is one of the most familiar passages in the Bible. It has been suggested that Dr. Luke interviewed Mary about Jesus' birth, and for this reason, Luke's account is so complete and incorporates Mary's thoughts about the whole event.

Our theme is obedience, and we have shown how Elizabeth and Zechariah were obedient and how Joseph and Mary obeyed by accepting what God had for them. Now we'll see these parents that God has picked for His Son obey the laws of Caesar.

The decree came at a very bad time! The ninth month of pregnancy is no time to go for a hike or even a donkey ride. But go they did! Mary and Joseph did not apply for a delay (there was no such thing); they did not cry and whine that God had mucked things up. They knew Scripture: the Messiah would be born in Bethlehem and since they were both from the line of David, to Bethlehem they would go. Mary packed the baby clothes; Joseph took a tool or two; and off they went.

They probably had to travel more slowly than their other relatives because of Mary's pregnancy, so when they arrived, everything was *full*. Now was that innkeeper a meany or was he kind? Well, a stable would certainly be warmer than a hillside camp spot. In Mary's song at Elizabeth's, she says, "His mercy extends to those who fear him." An innkeeper who probably wished he had an extra room extended God's mercy to them that night. But would shepherds have been intimidated by an inn? They certainly came eagerly to the stable!

The shepherds, too, were obedient to what God had to say. They "hurried off" to find the family in the stable.

Our Children are familiar with babies. Help them see this tiny baby snuggled warmly in the hay trough, not in a clean hospital or even a clean house.

New words to learn and review:

1. Messiah
2. Gospel
3. Manger – a box or trough to hold food for horses and cattle

Something to Make or Do:

1. Pictures to color and take home
2. Soup can pencil holders – wrap felt or other fabric around soup cans and glue it on. Decorate with sequins or felt cut-outs.
3. Christmas tree decorations of your choice.

Jesus Is Dedicated at the Temple

Scripture: Luke 2:21–39

Memory Verse: "Jesus said, 'Blessed (rather) are those who hear the word of God and obey it.'" Luke 11:28 (NIV)

Consider: I think I was almost an adult before I became familiar with this passage about Jesus' dedication at the Temple. Why? Perhaps because of the "hectic holidays," this one got lost in the shuffle. Many of our children have been formally dedicated to the Lord, and some of the children have seen a ceremony like this. So this is something they can relate to even if they can't completely understand the sacrifice part.

Several bits of information about Jesus' family can be gleaned from this passage:

1. They were not wealthy. The law said that for the purification of a woman after childbirth, they were to present a lamb unless they could not afford one, and then they could bring two doves or two pigeons (Leviticus 12:7–8).
2. They were obedient to the law. They went to the Temple to do what the law required.
3. They caused quite a stir when they brought Jesus in. Simeon rushed over and took the child in his arms and praised God. Anna spoke to all who were "looking forward to the redemption of Jerusalem."
4. They were amazed at what was said about the child.

Here again we see obedience.

- in Mary and Joseph – obedience to the law
- in Simeon – obedience to the Holy Spirit
- in Anna – obedience to the Holy Spirit

New words to learn and review:

1. Messiah
2. Gospel
3. Dedicate – to set apart seriously for a special purpose – to put into God's hands and care.

Something to make: Thumb print thank yous.

You'll need:

1. 1/2 sheets of 8 1/2 x 11 inch paper or writing tablet paper
2. water color paints
3. pens/pencils

Have the children dampen their thumbs in some water and then rub the dampened digit in the water color paint. Then they press their thumbs on the paper and clean off their thumbs. After the print has dried, they can make "bugs," "people," or whatever they want using the thumbprint as a center. These pieces of paper can then be used as stationery for Christmas thank yous.

The Wise Men and the Escape to Egypt

Scripture: Matthew 2

Memory Verse: "Jesus said, 'Blessed (rather) are those who hear the word of God and obey it.'" Luke 11:28 (NIV)

Consider: Scholars believe that this event occurred after Jesus was forty days old (presentation at the temple) and before he was two years old. The two years seem to indicate when the star appeared. We usually picture three wise men, but there may have been more. Certainly, three would not have started on a journey of 1,000 bandit-infested miles alone. They probably traveled with a caravan.

These men were of the learned class: advisors of kings. They had access to Herod, and their presence caused a bit of excitement in Jerusalem. Their coming demonstrated that Jesus was not just the King of the Jews, but that people from every tribe and nation should worship Him. They also provided the means of escape to Egypt. Mary and Joseph were not wealthy people. They did not have money to buy a hotel room when Jesus was born, and they didn't have enough money to provide a large sacrifice at the time of the dedication at the temple. God took care of the financial needs of His Son's family, and He will care for us, too.

The wise men obeyed when God told them not to go back to Herod. More obedience in this story.

Joseph obeyed immediately when the angel told him to take Mary and Jesus to Egypt. He obeyed again when the angel told him to go back to Israel, specifically Nazareth.

Our Children: The wise men probably caused as much of a stir in Bethlehem as they did in Jerusalem. Help our children see these men entering a humble home (even their own) in their jewels and rich robes. They brought wonderful gifts, too. The gifts each had significance:

Gold is the gift given to kings – Jesus is the KING;
Frankincense is the gift given to GOD – Jesus is GOD;
Myrrh is for preserving dead bodies – Jesus would die for us.

In the short run, the gifts helped Mary and Joseph escape. When our families travel, we need money for gas for our cars and food for our family members; or perhaps we use train or airplane tickets and hotels and restaurants. Have the children ask their parents about the expenses of traveling and moving to another place. God took care of Jesus and his family. He cares for our families, too.

New words to learn or review:

1. Gospel
2. Egypt is a country not far from Israel, but a hard trip on foot or donkey.

Something to Make or Do:

1. Act out the story. Perhaps starting with the Wise Men in their own countries getting ready and preparing gifts.

Jesus Grows Up and the Visit to the Temple

Scripture: Luke 2:41–52

Memory Verse: "Children, obey your parents in the Lord, for this is right." Ephesians 6:1 (NIV)

Consider: What would it have been like to have a child like Jesus? Mary and Joseph are the only ones who ever knew what it is like to have a child without a sin nature. The Bible tells us that Jesus was tempted in every way that we are, yet without sin. But He had to learn to do things just like our children do. When our boys were being potty trained I specifically asked Jesus to help the boys learn this because He had to learn it, too. He had to learn to read. I suspect His parents taught him to pray. In order to know and understand us, He had to *be* human, just as we are. He had to grow up.

And then there's the time at the Temple. At twelve, Jesus was beginning to understand Who He was. However, His timing was just a hair off. He wasn't really ready to begin His ministry, even if boys were considered adults at twelve (Bar Mitzvah). He was obedient to His parents!

Hebrews 5:8 tells us that "Although He was a Son, He learned obedience from the things which He suffered." We tend to equate the suffering with the events surrounding the crucifixion. However, we do not come to that sort of obedience without *lots* of practice.

Jesus learned obedience from the example of His earthly parents. He learned obedience from the disappointment of not being able to stay at the temple and learn when He was twelve. He learned obedience by having to wait until He was thirty years old to do the ministry God had sent Him to do. He learned through the suffering of the fast and we don't learn to fast for forty days by one day "doing it." He already knew how to fast! Yes, Jesus learned obedience just like we do.

Our Children: Who do the children know who is twelve? Help them see Jesus as a kid, a kid who got so wrapped up in being in the temple that He "forgot" to go home! Have the children's parents ever not known where they were? How frantic might Mary and Joseph have been?

New words to learn:

1. Temple – The huge building where the people worshiped God.

Something to Make or Do:

1. Act out the story

Jesus Is Baptized by John

Scripture: Matthew 3:13–17; Mark 1:9–11; Luke 3:21–22

Memory Verse: "Children, obey your parents in the Lord, for this is right." Ephesians 6:1 (NIV)

Consider: What is significant about Jesus being baptized at the same time as "all the people"? Is He identifying with us even though John's was a baptism of repentance, and Jesus had nothing to repent?

What three things happened at Jesus' baptism that made it unlike the others?

1. John resisted Jesus' coming to him for baptism. (Jesus had no need to repent.)
2. A voice from heaven said, "This is my beloved Son ..."
3. The Holy Spirit in the form of a dove landed on Him.

What meaning do you think these had for Jesus?

Jesus' baptism marked the beginning of His public ministry. Up to this time, John the Baptist had been preparing the way; at Jesus' baptism the focus shifts to Jesus.

Our Children: Some of the children have witnessed a baptism or have been baptized themselves. You and the children can describe the process for those who have not.

Some churches have built-in baptisteries, or they use the river or another body of water. In some traditions, people are baptized by having water sprinkled or poured over their heads. Some folks have been baptized in bathtubs. When children (other than infants) or adults are baptized, they are making an outward sign that they are identifying with Jesus and that they intend to follow Him.

New words to learn:

Baptize – baptism: When we are baptized, we are put under water in the name of the Father, Son, and Holy Spirit to

1. show that we believe that Jesus is our Savior,
2. show a cleansing and washing from sin, and
3. show a death to sin and a new life of righteous living.

Something to Make or Do:

1. Show photos or videos of people the children know being baptized.

Jesus Is Tempted

Scripture: Luke 4:1–12

Memory Verse: "Children, obey your parents in the Lord, for this is right." Ephesians 6:1 (NIV)

Consider: Many years ago, I was asked the question "Did Jesus know at the point of His baptism and temptation exactly who He was and what His mission would be?"

That is a complex question. When I was growing up, I was taught that Jesus knew what He knew because He was God, and we all know God knows everything. But this question made me think again. If Jesus is truly man, then He could not be God playing at being man; He had to be man. That meant that He, like us, could know in the Spirit but would function in faith.

Before the temptation, at Jesus' baptism, the heavens had opened, and God had spoken to Him. But Jesus had not yet done any miracles, nor had He had any formal public ministry. So when He's been fasting for forty days and is hungry, Satan comes along and asks Him to "test" that faith – "command that the stones be made bread." Satan tempted Jesus where He was vulnerable just like he does with us.

Think about it. I have never been tempted to pollute my body with tobacco products; however, I can be tempted to overindulge with chocolate sundaes. I might resist lying but might give in to gossip or grumbling! We tend to categorize sin and say that some sins are worse than others; God does not make those distinctions.

Our Children also have vulnerable points. Most of them will be tempted to ignore a parent's request in order to do what they want. They, like us, need to know that God will never let us be tempted above our capabilities; He will always provide a way of escape. (1 Corinthians 10:13 – "No temptation has seized you except what is common to man. And God is faithful; he will not let you be tempted beyond what you can bear. But when you are tempted, he will also provide a way out so that you can stand up under it.")

New words to learn:

1. Temptation/tempt: To test or try; to try to persuade someone to do something wrong or unwise; to make something inviting.

Something to Make or Do:

1. Draw a temptation and a child resisting
2. Role-play temptation and resisting

Jesus Calls the Disciples, part 1

Scripture: Matthew 1:18–21, (Mark 1:14–20 and Luke 5:1–11); Matthew 9:9–13 (Mark 2:13–17 and Luke 5:27).

Memory Verse: "Come, follow me," Jesus said, "and I will make you fishers of men." Matthew 4:19 (NIV)

Consider: This section can get confusing because some of the participants have two names. The disciple we usually refer to as Peter (the name Jesus gave him) is also called Simon and Cephas. Matthew is also known as Levi.

This lesson deals with the calling of the first five disciples: Peter and Andrew, James and John, and Matthew. The first four were fishermen, and Matthew was a tax collector. Did Jesus have a sense of humor or something? Fishermen and tax men! Jesus can use us all no matter what our occupations. Jesus asked these men to leave what they were doing to follow Him. They did. They immediately recognized in Jesus something, or someone they were looking for.

Jesus knew that as a man, He could not teach everyone, so He chose twelve to be with Him and be taught by Him. He invested three years of intense training into these men. He gave us a model for teaching – "Come along." The twelve watched Him, talked to Him, listened to Him, and learned from Him. When Jesus gave the command to "make disciples of all nations," I expect He wanted us to follow His pattern:

1. Take them along,
2. Teach them and show them how,
3. Let them try,
4. Regroup and answer questions, and
5. Empower them.

How can we do this?

Our Children will enjoy singing "I Will Make you Fishers of Men" as we help them understand what Jesus was asking of the disciples.

New words to learn:

1. Disciple – A disciple is a learner. When we speak of disciples in the biblical sense, we usually mean the twelve Jesus chose to be with Him. They would learn directly from Him for three years and then they would form the leadership of the church.

Something to Make or Do:

1. Act out the story.

Jesus Calls the Disciples, part 2

Scripture: "Come, follow me," Jesus said, "and I will make you fishers of men." Matthew 4:19 (NIV)

Consider: Jesus gave us a good example to follow: When He had an important decision to make, He spent much time in prayer.

Since Jesus was functioning as a man dependent on God while He was here on earth, He could know in the same way we know what we know in the Spirit. Jesus needed the guidance of the Father to know which men to choose to follow Him and be taught by Him. He spent the night in prayer and then called the twelve to Himself. Part of praying is listening to God speak to us.

Jesus chose twelve rather unlikely men to be companions for three years. God wanted to show that He uses people from all walks of life: fishermen, tax collectors, political zealots, and money handlers (Judas Iscariot held the purse – perhaps he had been a banker or investment counselor!)

Our Children need to see that God uses all of us in His service. One of the biggest errors Christians can make is to believe, and to perpetuate the belief, that some occupations are more holy and honorable than others. In many Christian circles, we exalt those in "full-time ministry" (pastors, missionaries, etc.).

These people have special responsibilities, true, but it does not mean that what they do is more important in the kingdom than what any other person does.

Identify those in the community who further the kingdom with their skills and talents. Not everyone is a pastor or teacher, but all can show God's love to those around them. (How about teachers in public schools who take Jesus to school with them each day? How about the person who fills the orders with a smile at the local fast food place?)

1 Corinthians 3:8–9 – "The man who plants and the man who waters have one purpose, and each will be rewarded according to his own labor. For we are God's fellow workers...."

Review:

Baptism
Temptation
Disciple
Gospel

Something to Make or Do:

1. Act out the story
2. Make valentines if appropriate

The Miracle at the Wedding

Scripture: John 2:1–11

Memory Verse: "For God so loved the word that he gave his one and only Son, that whoever believes in him shall not perish but have eternal life." John 3:16 (NIV)

Consider: Have you ever wondered why Jesus' first miracle was performed at a wedding and that basically His intervention kept the host from being embarrassed? It's probably not the way *we* might have begun a miracle ministry, but God's ways are not our ways.

The wedding was a happy occasion. Mary was present; the disciples were there. Family and friends. What was Jesus' message throughout His ministry? The kingdom of heaven is at hand. The kingdom of heaven is like…. In this instance, the kingdom is a joyous place with family, friends, food, and drink.

The jars Jesus filled with wine were not the sort we might buy at the local grocery store. These were huge jars, each holding twenty to thirty *gallons*! When Jesus supplied wine, He supplied it in abundance. The Bible says there were six of these jars. That's 120–180 *gallons* of wine!

Our Children may or may not have been to a large wedding. Let's help them see that a wedding is a joyous occasion where we usually invite all our friends and relatives. It takes a lot of food to feed a crowd like that, even if it's only cake, nuts, and mints. Running out of food or punch at a party like that would be a major embarrassment for the host. Jesus fixed the problem and gave the servants and the disciples a hint at who He was.

New words to learn:

1. Wedding – a ceremony in which a man and a woman marry each other. (Bring pictures of weddings and wedding food if possible.)
2. Perish – die

Something to Make or Do:

1. Valentines, if appropriate
2. Act out the story

Nicodemus Meets Jesus

Scripture: John 3:1–20

Memory Verse: "Come, follow me," Jesus said, "and I will make you fishers of men." Matthew 4:19 (NIV)

Consider: Nicodemus was a member of the Sanhedrin – the Jewish Supreme Court. He was interested in what Jesus was teaching and doing, and he went to Jesus privately to ask Him questions. Whatever Nicodemus believed about Jesus at this point, we know that later, he and Joseph of Arimathea buried Jesus. That took considerable courage since the Jewish leaders all seemed to be against Jesus.

Our Children can understand the idea of the new birth. We are body, soul, and spirit, and the part of us that gets contaminated by sin needs to be reborn.

In our day, the term "born again" has probably been misused and over-used until it has little meaning to the general population. Our little ones, however, may or may not have heard this term, and it can help them understand what happens when Jesus comes into their lives in this way.

The Bible does not declare that children are condemned to hell if they have not had a new birth experience. Eventually, they must make their own decisions about what they will do with Jesus, but

many are not ready to do so at this time. However, some *are* ready. Children who are raised in the Word by loving, praying parents naturally love Jesus. A book I have found very helpful in this regard is called *Kids and the Kingdom* by John Inchly and published by Tyndale House. It is out of print but can be found through inter-library loan or through Tyndale House.

Review:

Gospel
Messiah
Baptism
Perish

Something to Make or Do:

1. Butterflies (new birth) – Refrigerator magnets made with clothespins, magnet strips, construction paper, and pipe cleaners.
Cut the construction paper into the shape of wings. Let the children color or decorate them. Then glue the wings to the clothespin. The pipe cleaners can be glued to the pin with a glue gun or white glue. Magnet strips – available in craft stores – are glued to the back of the clothespin.
2. Butterfly pictures

Jesus and the Samaritan Woman at the Well

Scripture: John 4:1–42

Memory Verse: "Come, follow me," Jesus said, "and I will make you fishers of men." Matthew 4:19 (NIV)

Consider: This woman came to the well at an unusual hour, probably because the other women in the town wouldn't have anything to do with her. She had a bad reputation. She had had five husbands and was living with a man who was not her husband. Why might Jesus ask a favor of her?

Notice how the woman changes the subject and tries to entangle Jesus in the religious controversy of the day. Has that ever happened to you? Have you ever done it? How does Jesus get her back on track?

Jesus stayed in town for two days because the people wanted to hear what He had to say. At first, they believed because of what the woman said. Then they believed because of what Jesus said!

Our Children may have been told they should not play with certain children in their neighborhoods, or they don't want to play with some because they are trouble-makers. A lot in the Bible indicates that is a good idea. But we also need to see that Jesus loves those people, too. And when they believe, great changes occur in their lives.

New words to learn:

1. Samaria/Samaritan: People from the town of Samaria. They were not Jews or they were mixed Jews. They believed in God and some of them kept the law. Since many Jews got into sin problems when they mixed with the Samaritans, most Jews avoided the Samaritans.

Something to Make or Do:

1. Draw "I can show I care by …"
2. Make a gift for someone.

Spring Quarter

Jesus Is our Teacher and Savior.

SUGGESTION: You might want to use a Bible Story Book for this one. This is a complex story.

Memory work for this quarter:

Week 1–3 The Lord's Prayer from Matthew 6:9 KJV

Our Father which art in heaven, Hallowed be thy name. Thy kingdom come. Thy will be done in earth, as it is in heaven. Give us this day our daily bread. And forgive us our debts (trespasses), as we forgive our debtors (those who trespass against us). And lead us not into temptation, but deliver us from evil: For thine is the kingdom, and the power, and the glory, forever. Amen.

Weeks 4–5: "For the Son of Man came to seek and save what was lost."

—Luke 19:10, NIV

Weeks 6–8: "If you love me, you will obey what I command. And I will ask the Father, and he will give you another Counselor to be with you forever – the Spirit of truth."

—John 14:15–16, NIV

Weeks 9–10: Jesus said to Thomas, "… Because you have seen me, you have believed; blessed are those who have not seen and yet have believed."

—John 20:29, NIV

Weeks 11–13: "Therefore go and make disciples of all nations, baptizing them in the name of the Father and of the Son, and of the Holy Spirit…."

—Matthew 28:19, NIV

Spring Quarter

Spring finds us in the Easter season. The focus of the lessons for this quarter is Jesus as our teacher and Savior.

Many people addressed Jesus as "Rabbi" or teacher. As an itinerant rabbi, Jesus proclaimed that the "kingdom is at hand" and often, "the kingdom is like…." In the first lessons, we see Jesus teaching the disciples how to pray. I'm sure they already knew something about prayer, but they had been observing their teacher closely, and they saw that His prayers seemed to give Him something extra. Thus, we have the prayer which gives us a pattern to follow.

The next three lessons involve stories that Jesus told. The parable is a narrative form which uses fictional elements to teach a concept. (The use of the term "fiction" here is in the literary sense: imaginative.) Just prior to the telling of the Good Samaritan story, a Pharisee asked, "And who is my neighbor?" Jesus could have pulled out his *Webster's Dictionary* and given the man the definition. Instead, He told a story, and from that story, we can "see" what a neighbor is in quite a memorable way. Had Jesus given a dictionary definition, the hearers would have promptly forgotten, and we would not have the classic story.

From there, we move to the events surrounding the crucifixion and resurrection. Jesus is our Savior – the one Who saves us from sin and eternal death. Even here, we see Jesus teaching His followers. On the road to Emmaus, He opens the prophets to them so they can understand what has happened. He teaches forgiveness and restoration to one who denied Him. He sends the Holy Spirit Who will lead them into all truth.

Lord, Teach Us to Pray

Scripture: Matthew 6:5–14; Luke 11:1–4

Memory Verse: The Lord's Prayer (We will work on this for several weeks. Send a copy home with the children so they can work on this with their parents.)

Our Father, Who art in Heaven,

Hallowed be Thy Name.

Thy kingdom come;

Thy will be done on earth as it is in Heaven.

Give us this day our daily bread,

And forgive us our debts (trespasses) as we forgive our debtors (those who trespass against us).

And lead us not into temptation, but deliver us from evil.

For Thine is the kingdom, and the power, and the glory forever.

Amen. (traditional)

Consider: The Lord's Prayer is simple and profound. It contains the elements of prayer that Jesus had learned were important.

1. Recognition of Who God is – Our heavenly Father
2. Recognition of God's attribute of holiness – Hallowed be Thy Name …
3. Affirmation of our loyalty to God – Thy kingdom come … Heaven.
4. Conscious dependency on God – Give us this day …
5. Confession/relational healing – Forgive us our debts …

6. Strength for the spiritual battle – Lead us not into temptation
7. Praise – For Thine is the kingdom … Amen (While this section does not appear in Matthew or in Luke, it is derived from 1 Chronicles 29:11: "Thine, O LORD is the greatness, and the power, and the glory, and the victory, and the majesty: for all that is in the heaven and in the earth is thine; thine is the kingdom, O LORD, and thou art exalted as head above all." (KJV)

Our Children should have no trouble learning this prayer if taken by bits and if repeated for several weeks. We all learn in patterns, and when we know the pattern, the rest falls into place. Jesus taught a "patterned" prayer so we could not only recite the one He gave, but we could use that pattern at other times in our lives.

New words to learn or review:

1. Gospel – a. The good news about Jesus
   b. The first four books of the New Testament
2. Disciple – a learner – in this story, the twelve particular men Jesus called to be with Him and to learn from Him.
3. Prayer – talking to God

Something to Make or Do:

1. Make a small "Bible Book" with verses relating to prayer
2. A prayer list

The Wise and Foolish Builders

Scripture: Matthew 7:24–29

Memory Verse: The Lord's Prayer

> Our Father, Who art in Heaven,
>
> Hallowed be Thy Name.
>
> Thy kingdom come;
>
> Thy will be done on earth as it is in Heaven.
>
> Give us this day our daily bread,
>
> And forgive us our debts (trespasses) as we forgive our debtors (those who trespass against us.)
>
> And lead us not into temptation, but deliver us from evil.
>
> For Thine is the kingdom, and the power, and the glory forever.
>
> Amen. (traditional)

Consider: In this unit, we are dealing with the idea that Jesus is our Teacher. This particular section of Scripture is not really a parable, but it is an analogy – a comparison which helps us to understand the message that the teacher is communicating. In the comparison of the builders, Jesus uses an example that the ordinary people of His day would understand. Two builders, two houses. One house is built on sand, and the other is built on a rock. The teachings of Jesus are like the rock. They are solid and sure. When we follow what He says, we find our lives in "good shape." But when we ignore what He says, our lives crumble.

Our Children will enjoy this story and the little song that tells the story.

"The Wise Man and the Foolish Man" by Ann Omley, 1948

1. The wise man built his house upon the Rock,
   The wise man built his house upon the Rock,
   The wise man built his house upon the Rock,
   And the rains came tumbling down.
   The rains came down and the floods came up,
   The rains came down and the floods came up,
   The rains came down and the floods came up,
   But the house on the Rock stood firm.

2. The foolish man built his house upon the sand,
   The foolish man built his house upon the sand,
   The foolish man built his house upon the sand,
   And the rains came tumbling down.
   The rains came down and the floods came up,
   The rains came down and the floods came up,
   The rains came down and the floods came up,
   And the house on the sand fell flat.

3. So build your life on the Lord Jesus Christ,
   So build your life on the Lord Jesus Christ,
   So build your life on the Lord Jesus Christ,
   And the blessings will come down.
   The blessings come down as your prayers go up,
   The blessings come down as your prayers go up,
   The blessings come down as your prayers go up,
   So build your life on the Lord.

New words to learn or review:

1. Gospel – a. The good news about Jesus
   b. The first four books of the New Testament
2. Disciple – a learner – in this story, the twelve particular men Jesus called to be with Him and to learn from Him.
3. Prayer – talking to God

Something to Make or Do:

1. Demonstrate building on sand and rocks. Put some sand in the bottom of a plastic tub and then place a large flat rock in the sand. Create little houses with plastic play bricks or popsicle sticks. Set one house on the sand and one on the rock. Pour water (gently) over the house on the sand. The sand is likely to shift and the house will not stay put. Then pour water (gently) over the house on the rock. (Or you might glue the house to the rock.) The rock will not shift under the house like the sand did.

The Good Samaritan

Scripture: Luke 10:25–37

Memory Verse: Continue work on the Lord's Prayer.

Consider: This story of the Good Samaritan is one of the most famous of Jesus' parables. He told it in response to a question: "Who is my neighbor?"

Old Testament law (Leviticus 21:1–4) said that the priests should not touch a dead body and make themselves ceremonially unclean. So when the priest and the religious Levite saw the man half dead (and dead for all they knew), they decided not to get involved. Jesus' audience was, no doubt, expecting that the third person would be an ordinary Jew. However, the great teacher gave the story a twist they did not expect and made the neighbor a hated Samaritan. It was a startling turn, and it made the listeners perk up their ears.

Our Children love this story. They can learn from it just as we can. The priest and the Levite might have had good reasons to avoid the injured man. But they didn't even stop. The person who helped was a hated Samaritan. What acts of kindness can *they* perform? Preschoolers and Primaries are not noted for their kindness nor their sensitivity to others' needs. But they can learn.

Children can help Mom and Dad by picking up toys and clothes without whining. They can brush or feed pets. They can play with younger siblings. They can show concern for those who are hurting.

This is a good story for the children to act out. They can take turns being the injured man, the priest, the Levite, and the Samaritan.

New words to learn:

1. Parable – A story told to teach a truth. [I learned the definition of parable as an "earthly story with a heavenly meaning."] Jesus used parables to link a real-life situation with the heavenly principle or truth he was trying to convey. Those who had ears to hear, would hear.

Something to Make or Do:

1. "Kindness chart" – or "kindness coupons"
2. Act out the story

The Prodigal Son

Scripture: Luke 15:11–31

Memory Verse: "For the Son of Man came to seek and save what was lost." Luke 19:10 (NIV)

Consider: The way Luke has organized this section, we see the story of the lost son as the culmination in a series of "lost" things. First is the lost sheep. Okay, they all knew that sheep got lost. Second is the dowry coin. "Sure, my wife lost one of those last week." And then there is the lost son. The progression is from ho-hum to wow.

We can look at this parable from several angles. From one angle, the story is about a foolish young man who decides that home is just too dull, and he must go off into the world if he is to have any fun. Do you suppose his father knew what he would do? Certainly. We don't live with our children to adulthood and not know their characters. Perhaps he is like someone we know. He had good teaching as a child but decided he knew best and went off to make his way in the world. He eventually realized there was no real joy there and returned home.

From another angle, it is about a loving father who has done his best, but when the younger son presses the father for his share of the inheritance, the father reluctantly gives in, knowing that his hard-earned cash will be wasted. He anticipates his son's return, however, and sees him coming from a long way off. He rejoices that his son has returned – just as God rejoices when we come home to Him.

From another perspective, it is about a dutiful son (again, perhaps someone we know) who is angry and hurt when the prodigal is restored to the family. Can we learn to rejoice with God when a lost one returns? Is there forgiveness and restoration?

Our Children can understand this simple story. Years ago, Pat Boone recorded a parody of the Prodigal Son in a story called "Antshillvania." Our guys still remember some of the lines from that one. Maybe a child has wandered away in a store and remembers how glad Mom and Dad were when he or she was restored! This is a great one to act out.

Help our kids learn that God is like the kind father who watched for his son and welcomed him home.

New words to learn or review:

1. Parable – A story told to teach a truth. [I learned the definition of parable as an "earthly story with a heavenly meaning."] Jesus used parables to link a real-life situation with the heavenly principle or truth He was trying to convey. Those who had ears to hear, would hear.

Something to Make or Do:

Act out the story

The People Praise Jesus

Scripture: Matthew 21:1–11

Memory Verse: "For the Son of Man came to seek and save what was lost." Luke 19:10 (NIV)

Consider: When I was a child, I thought that Jesus knew about the little donkey being tied up because He was God. While that is true, it is not the whole story. Jesus called himself the "Son of Man." He lived life as a man. He kept in touch with the Father just as we should. He went alone to pray as we should. He studied Scripture just as we should. He exercised the gifts of the Spirit just as we should. Here, He was probably exercising the word of knowledge just as we could.

When Jesus entered Jerusalem on that day, the people hailed Him as "David's son," the one Who "comes in the name of the Lord." And truly He came in the name of the Lord. He went to the Temple and again threw out those who were buying and selling there. (John tells us He did that early in His ministry, too.) And then He healed the blind and the lame. The people praised Him, but that made the authorities angry! Are we like the teachers of the law? Or are we like the children who offered perfect praise?

Our Children love parades! And Jesus was a parade all by Himself. The children waved palm branches and sang Hosanna! When we lived in Indonesia, it was the custom to lay palm branches in the aisle of the church on Palm Sunday. What a racket they made! So not only were the crowds yelling and praising God, the donkey was crunching along on the palm branches. Can you imagine the noise?

New words to learn or review:

1. Palm Sunday – One week before Easter. We celebrate this as the day Jesus rode into Jerusalem in triumph. Children singing Hosanna!

Something to Make or Do:

1. Palm branches to wave. Act out the story.

Jesus Prays for Us (the Garden of Gethsemane)

Scripture: Matthew 26:36–46 and John 17

Memory Verse: "If you love me, you will obey what I command. And I will ask the Father, and he will give you another Counselor to be with you forever – the Spirit of truth." John 14:15–16 (NIV)

Consider: Have you ever noticed the great teaching that Jesus did between the Upper Room and the Garden of Gethsemane? Jesus knew He had a very little time, and He needed to say what He had to say. Would they remember it all? Yes, the Holy Spirit, the comforter and counselor, would remind them.

Then there's the Garden. Imagine you are a disciple. You've just had a big holiday meal and a long walk. You'd like to pray with the Master; the kingdom is coming and you know it. Jesus has just been talking about "going away." Sure, you're curious, but you're also sleepy. And you just cannot stay awake! I'm glad somebody was at least half awake, though, or we wouldn't have the transcript of Jesus' prayer. We wouldn't know how human He was at that point. "My Father, if it is possible, may this cup be taken from me…." (Matthew 26:39). But we also see that He was able to overcome the part of Him that would bolt! "My Father, if it is not possible for this cup to be taken away unless I drink it, may your will be done" (Matthew 26:42).

John tells us how He prayed for the disciples, not only the twelve that God "gave (Him) out of the world" (John 17:6), but for us. "My prayer is not for them alone. I pray also for those who will believe in me through their message, that all of them may be one …" Jesus prayed for us that night in the Garden when He sweat drops of blood. He also prayed for the children we teach and their families. He prayed for those in prisons – through their own fault or the fault of governments.

Our Children can find this lesson encouraging just as we can. Jesus was very sad, and yet He could see beyond the present suffering to "those who would believe." Can we help the children see beyond the end of their noses?

New words to learn or review:

1. Gethsemane: the name of the Garden where Jesus prayed before He was arrested.

Something to Make or Do:

1. Plant seeds or cuttings (need potting soil, clear plastic drinking cups, seeds or cuttings, water, lots of newspapers or plastic bags.

The Crucifixion and Resurrection

Scripture: Matthew 26:47 – 28:20; Mark 15:1–16:8; Luke 22:47–24:12; John 18:1–20:18.

Suggestion: You might use a Bible story book for this one. This is a complex story.

Memory Verse: "If you love me, you will obey what I command. And I will ask the Father, and he will give you another Counselor to be with you forever – the Spirit of truth." John 14:15–16

Consider: This is the most important event in history! If it were not for the crucifixion *and* the resurrection, we would not be able to enter into a relationship with God. It is the resurrection that gives us hope. We serve a living God.

Our Children: Although this section of Scripture is complex with Jesus being traipsed off here and there during the night, the message is a simple one. "Jesus died and lives again." All the rest is detail! Details we can learn from, of course. The tomb is empty. The children may or may not have experienced death in their lives (death of grandparent, pet, friend, etc.) and so they may not understand the permanency of death. But the idea here is that Jesus conquered death! He lives.

You may have many resources to teach this lesson: pictures, flannel graphs, etc. Choose the ones that will work best with the children.

New words to learn or review:

1. Resurrection: coming to life again after being dead. This is what we celebrate at Easter.
2. Crucifixion: A method of executing (putting to death) criminals.

Something to Make or Do:

1. Cross bookmarks
2. An activity that involves some work but can have a huge impact is to create a "stations of the cross" for the children. Depending on facilities, you could have a "last supper," a "walk" to the garden; a trip to the Sanhedrin and a stop with Pilate; a hike up Calvary; and a peek into the empty tomb. Use your Bible and your imagination.

Jesus Meets Friends on the Road to Emmaus

Scripture: Luke 24:13–35 (also Luke 24:36–49)

Memory Verse: "If you love me, you will obey what I command. And I will ask the Father, and he will give you another Counselor to be with you forever – the Spirit of truth." John 14:15–16

Consider: Have you ever had an experience like the one Jesus' followers had? Someone you know (or have known) comes up to you, walks and talks with you, and you don't recognize the person. Most of us eventually recognize the person within a few moments, but Cleopas and his companion don't recognize Jesus! I wonder why. Maybe God shut their eyes. Maybe, because they believed Jesus to be dead, they did not expect to see Him, and they did not. Maybe carrying the sins of the world for those hours on the cross changed His physical appearance so much that He was unrecognizable! That's one we can ask when we get to heaven!

The two followers were still thinking of Jesus in terms of an earthly kingdom: "And we had hoped He would be the one Who was going to set Israel free!" And they pondered the women's reports of the resurrection. Should they believe or not? Do we ever do this? Do we doubt God's moving? In any case, Jesus scolded them for not believing: "How slow you are to believe everything the prophets said!" But He didn't leave it there. He "explained to them what was said about Himself in all the Scriptures, beginning with the books of Moses and the writings

of all the prophets." No doubt He was realigning their thinking about the nature of the Kingdom.

It's interesting that Cleopas and his companion recognized Jesus when He broke the bread. They had eaten with Him many times; perhaps He had a characteristic gesture that gave Him away to them.

Then they hurried back to Jerusalem! In the dark! And while they were telling their experience to the apostles, Jesus appeared again and they were terrified! Again He chides them but does not quit with the chiding; He again explains His purpose!

Let us be encouraged! He may chide us, but He is patient and will explain it all again until we understand and believe. Jesus is our teacher – let's follow His example.

Our Children could have fun acting this one out. Find some (three or four will probably do) references to Jesus' sufferings in the Old Testament (Isaiah is a good place to look) and coach "Jesus" with His lines. All the kids can participate because we can have a group of "apostles," "Jesus," and the two followers.

New words to learn and review:

1. Resurrection: coming to life again after being dead.

Something to Make or Do:

1. Have the children draw the different parts of the story and then hang the pictures on the wall.

The Upper Room/ Thomas Believes

Scripture: John 20:19–31

Memory Verse: "Jesus said to Thomas, "… Because you have seen me, you have believed; blessed are those who have not seen and yet have believed." John 20:29 (NIV)

Consider: Thomas was not one to be taken in by hysterical women or "gullible" fishermen and tax collectors. He would not believe unless he saw Jesus for himself! He didn't want to be disappointed again! How many times are we like that? We want concrete proof!

It is interesting that Jesus does not scold Thomas. When Jesus appears, He simply calls Thomas forward to touch the nail scars. He instructs him to "Stop doubting and believe." Jesus gave Thomas what he needed to believe – just as He gives us what we need to believe.

Critics have said that the teaching of the resurrection grew out of the disciples' imaginations. However, over and over, we see that those closest to Jesus did not believe He was alive. Remember, a guard was posted by the tomb because the leaders remembered that He said He'd rise again. Perhaps those outside of Jesus' circle believed more than the disciples!

Our Children can believe, too. But we must remember they are at an age when the line between fantasy and reality is very thin. They can believe in Jesus' resurrection, and they can believe in a magical Easter Bunny. At this age, let's not worry about the Easter Bunny (or Santa Claus) and emphasize the reality of the resurrection!

New words to learn or review:

1. Gospel – a. The good news about Jesus' resurrection
   b. The first four books of the New Testament.

Something to Make or Do:

1. Make a card for someone.

Jesus and the Miraculous Catch of Fish

Scripture: John 21: 1–14

Memory Verse: Jesus said to Thomas, "… Because you have seen me, you have believed; blessed are those who have not seen and yet have believed." John 20:29 (NIV)

Consider: The disciples were probably feeling perplexed. They didn't know yet what they were to do with the training that Jesus had given them. He was crucified, but He had risen and was now alive. So what were they to *do* besides believe? So Peter and some of the others decided to go fishing. It was something they knew. It was familiar.

All night they fished and caught nothing. Then at sunrise, they saw someone walking along the water's edge. And they shouted back and forth about the bad fishing. Then Jesus told them to put the net on the right side of the boat. They didn't know it was Jesus, but they did it anyway. What had they to lose? Maybe they wondered if it was Jesus. We are not told. However, as soon as the nets were full, they *knew*: "It is the Lord!"

They pulled the nets ashore and even though the nets were very full, they did not break! As the disciples came near, they saw that Jesus had cooked breakfast for them. Some have suggested that this may have been near where Jesus originally asked them to follow Him, thus making it symbolic, calling again. It's interesting to speculate, but we don't know.

Our Children will probably enjoy singing a song I learned in my youth which can be accessed in several formats online.

Peter, James, and John in a sailboat – 3x
Out on the deep blue sea.

New words to learn and review:

1. Gospel – a. The good news about Jesus' resurrection
   b. The first four books of the New Testament.

Something to Make or Do:

1. Have a "breakfast" of fish.

Jesus Forgives Peter

Scripture: John 21:15–25

Memory Verse: "Therefore go and make disciples of all nations, baptizing them in the name of the Father and of the Son, and of the Holy Spirit ..." Matthew 28:19

Consider: Peter has seen Jesus at least twice since the Resurrection. Jesus hasn't singled him out in any way. Perhaps he knows Jesus has forgiven him. But the rest of the disciples know about the denial. What is Jesus going to do about that? Think about a time when there has been uneasiness between you and a friend. You seem to be dancing around each other, waiting for the other to speak of the tiff. I suppose that's how Peter felt. He wanted to make everything right with Jesus again, and some things needed to be aired in a public way. But he wasn't sure how – or if it was even his move.

Jesus made the move. He asked Peter outright: "Do you love me more than these?" Peter dances around this a bit, and Jesus asks him three times, "Do you love me?"

"You know all things, and You know I love You," says Peter. Because Peter had bragged that he would never deny Jesus and then did so, royally, the restoration had to be done publicly. Jesus says, "Feed my sheep." Peter is restored. Peter has been given a job to do, and Jesus would not entrust "feeding" to someone untrustworthy.

Our Children will like to know that Jesus forgave Peter for denying Him. It helps them know that He forgives us, too, when we sin.

New words to learn and review:

1. Forgive: to give up resentment against or the desire to punish; to stop being angry with someone.

Something to make:

1. Mothers' Day projects – "handprints" – cards, bookmarks.
    Print the following poem on pieces of paper. Then trace the children's hands on the paper. This makes a great Mom's Day present.

Poem for Handprints

Fingerprints

I know you get discouraged
Because I am so small
And always leave my fingerprints
On furniture and walls.

But every day I'm growing,
I'll be all grown up someday,
And all the smudges that I did
Will surely fade away.

So here's another bunch of them
Just so you can recall
Exactly how my fingers looked
When I was very small.

Wendy Lyn

Jesus Goes Back to Heaven

Scripture: Luke 24:50–52, Acts 1:7–11

Memory Verse: "Therefore go and make disciples of all nations, baptizing them in the name of the Father and of the Son, and of the Holy Spirit …" Matthew 28:19

Consider: Jesus had been appearing to the disciples and other followers off and on for forty days. Now He was going to the Father. He instructed the disciples to stay in Jerusalem until the Holy Spirit came upon them. If they had left town immediately, without the Spirit, the Good News might have been lost, and they would not have had the impact that they had on the whole area. God continues to renew us publicly – perhaps so there is a united impact on our communities.

Our Children are becoming disciples. Part of the Gospel story is that Jesus ascended into heaven and intercedes for us with the Father. Jesus told His followers to wait for the Holy Spirit. We often want the power *now*, thank you. But God, in His wisdom, sometimes asks us to wait until He is ready and until *we* are ready. I suspect the followers spent the next ten days (till Pentecost) praying and studying Scripture. What did Jesus mean? Who is the Holy Spirit? What did Jesus have to say about the Spirit? When Pentecost came, they were ready. Peter knew that *this* was what Joel had written about. We can help our children be ready, too.

New words to learn and review:

1. Ascension: comes from the word ascend, which mean to go up. Jesus went up into heaven in a cloud.

Something to Make or Do:

1. Role-play "studying" about the Holy Spirit. What do the children/disciples already know?

Jesus Sends the Holy Spirit

Scripture: Acts 2:1–42

Memory Verse: "Therefore go and make disciples of all nations, baptizing them in the name of the Father and of the Son, and of the Holy Spirit …" Matthew 28:19

Consider: The followers of Jesus – at least 120 of them – went back to Jerusalem after the Ascension, and Acts 1:14 tells us that they "gathered frequently to pray as a group." Ten days later (Pentecost), when they gathered to pray, the Holy Spirit came with a loud rush of wind, tongues of fire sat above their heads, and they were all filled with the Holy Spirit.

In their amazement and joy, they moved outside. Because of the commotion, they drew a crowd. Each person in the crowd heard the message of the Messiahship of Christ in his or her own language. Many interpretations are given here. Perhaps each disciple spoke another language. Perhaps the Holy Spirit acted as interpreter. Some commentators understand this event as different from "speaking in tongues," glossolalia, which is unintelligible until interpreted. I'm not sure it really matters. What matters is that the church was born, and 3,000 people believed and were baptized!

Our Children may have seen and some may have participated in a movement of the Spirit. They can understand this story about the beginnings of the church. When Peter addressed the crowd, he spoke of the Old Testament Scriptures. He had studied, and they had studied. Peter was able to link the Old Testament and the recent events in Jerusalem so that people could believe.

Yes, we need that special touch from the Spirit. But we also need to know how to relate what we experience to what God has said and to what others have experienced. Let's give our kids both the experience and the knowledge!

New words to learn and review:

1. Pentecost: means fiftieth and is the Greek word for the Feast of (seven) Weeks described in Lev. 23:15–22, which was celebrated at the end of the harvest. In other words, this was a feast time and many extra people were in Jerusalem. So many more people heard the message than might have otherwise.

Something to Make or Do:

1. Act out the story.

Summer Quarter

Lesson 1 to 4

The Armor of God

Scripture: Ephesians 6:10–18

Memory Verse: The children will have plenty of time to learn this as the "armor" lessons cover several weeks. Ephesians 6:13–18

Consider: Children need the armor of God if they are to "stand against the devil's schemes" and be the light and salt Jesus wants them to be in their world. We can ask for God's protection over them, and He will protect them. But there will come a time when they must do battle, and they will need the "whole armor of God."

Overview: This is designed to be a very active sort of unit. The study is Ephesians 6:10–18, and during the four weeks, the children will

1. Memorize the Scripture verses,
2. Learn the various parts of the armor and how they relate to the Roman soldiers' armor, and

3. Learn how each spiritual counterpart protects the soldier of God.
4. They will also construct "armor" out of cardboard, aluminum foil, milk jugs, etc.

Lesson 1: Intro and Belt of Truth

Lesson 2: Breastplate of Righteousness

       Shoes of the readiness to announce the Gospel of peace

Lesson 3: Shield of Faith

       Helmet of Salvation

Lesson 4: Sword of the Spirit Prayer

They will construct the belt of truth, the breastplate, the shield, the helmet and the sword.

Directions are available on the web at http://www.instructables.com/id/Roman-esque-soldier-uniform – from-cardboard!

The Armor of God (belt of truth)

Scripture: Ephesians 6:10–18

Memory Verse: Ephesians 6:13–18 "Therefore put on the full armor of God, so that when the day of evil comes, you may be able to stand your ground, and after you have done everything, to stand. Stand firm then, with the belt of truth buckled around your waist, with the breastplate of righteousness in place, and with your feet fitted with the readiness that comes from the gospel of peace. In addition to all this, take up the shield of faith, with which you can extinguish all the flaming arrows of the evil one. Take the helmet of salvation and the sword of the Spirit, which is the word of God. And pray in the Spirit on all occasions with all kinds of prayers and requests. With this in mind, be alert and always keep on praying for all the Lord's people." (NIV)

The children will have several weeks to learn this important Scripture. This is a long passage, and you'll find it divided into sections. For example, older children could learn the whole thing while younger ones could learn just the armor pieces.

In this lesson, the children will be introduced to the Roman soldier and his armor. When the soldier went into battle, he needed protection from the swords, lances, and arrows of the enemy. In the book of Ephesians, Paul gives instructions for family living and personal warfare.

> … (B)e strong in the Lord and in his mighty power. Put on the full armor of God so that you can take your stand against the devil's schemes. For our struggle is not against flesh and blood, but against the rulers, against the authorities, against the powers of this dark world and against the spiritual forces of evil in the heavenly realms. Therefore, put on the full armor of God, so that when the day of evil comes, you may be able to stand your ground, and after you have done everything, to stand.
>
> —Ephesians 6:10–13, NIV

Start the memory work here:

> Put on the full armor of God, so that when the day of evil comes, you may be able to stand your ground, and after you have done everything, to stand.
>
> —Ephesians 6:13

What are the schemes of the devil? (lies, deception – remember Adam and Eve; accuser of the brethren – Rev. 12:10). Actually, I think he sticks pretty close to lies and deception. He twists the truth – as he did in the Garden of Eden and with Jesus in the wilderness. He's not above using Scripture. He appears as an angel of light (2 Corinthians 11:14) so we are deceived into believing that what he says is good.

There is defensive/protective armor:

1. Belt of truth. The Roman soldier's belt didn't hold up his pants. He wore a short tunic. The belt covered the part of his body that wasn't protected by much bone. From the belt hung strips of armor to protect his vulnerable organs, and it held his short sword.

New words to learn or review:

1. Truth is sincerity and honesty; agreement with the facts; accuracy. Truth protects the soldier of God and is his defense. Some of the older children may remember a time when they met up with a lie about themselves or someone they know. Or they may remember a time when they were tempted to lie but told the truth and the

situation turned out well. As adults, we can move in confidence when we move in truth. Jesus said that we can know the truth and the truth can set us free.

When we know the truth of what God says, then we are protected from the lies of the devil.

Something to Make or Do:

1. The belt of truth could be made from cloth strips tied around the children's waists. The "armor" could be pieces of cloth or cardboard stapled to the belt. Belts could be tied or pinned.
2. The picture of the Roman soldier to color to remind the children of the armor parts.

An internet search of "Roman soldier's armor" should yield some great results. I'd suggest spending some time working on the memory work. Send the verses home, so the children can work on them at home.

The Armor of God (breastplate and shoes)

This week we look at more defensive/protective armor: the breastplate of righteousness and the shoes of readiness to preach the Gospel.

Scripture: Ephesians 6:13–18

Memory Verse: "Stand firm then, with the belt of truth buckled around your waist, with the breastplate of righteousness in place, and with your feet fitted with the readiness that comes from the gospel of peace." Ephesians 6:14, 15

Consider:

Breastplate of righteousness: The Roman soldier wore a breastplate to protect the upper part of his body from enemy weapons. It covered his heart among other things.

Righteousness: Right, honorable, just.

When we "wear" righteousness, we may get shot at, but the arrows are deflected. Justice and honor set apart the soldier of God from others.

But I say to you, love your enemies, and pray for those who persecute you in order that you may be sons of your Father who is in heaven; for He causes His sun to rise on the evil and the good, and sends rain on the righteous and the unrighteous. For if you love those who love you, what reward have you? Do not even the tax gatherers do the same:

And if you greet your brothers only, what do you do more than others? Do not even the Gentiles do the same?—Matthew 5:44

When we wear truth and righteousness, we can go confidently into battle.

[Breastplates can be made of cardboard and tied on with strips of fabric or shoelaces.]

Shoes are protective. They protect our feet as we go to take the Good News to others. It may be that we go across the street or across town or to the other side of the world. And when we go, we should take peace (God's peace) with us.

A soldier who loved God: Cornelius. His story is found in Acts 10.

New words to learn or review:

1. Truth is sincerity and honesty; agreement with the facts; accuracy.
2. Righteousness: Right, honorable, just.

Something to Make or Do:

1. Picture of the Roman soldier if they haven't already done it.
2. Breastplate – cardboard, decorated, tied on.
3. Start shields.

Armor of God (shield of faith and helmet of salvation)

We have more defensive/protective armor this week: shield of faith and helmet of salvation.

Scripture: Ephesians 6:10–18. A soldier who loved God: a Roman centurion with a sick servant. His story is found in Luke 7.

Memory Verse: "In addition to all this, take up the shield of faith, with which you can extinguish all the flaming arrows of the evil one. Take the helmet of salvation and the sword of the Spirit, which is the word of God." Ephesians 6:16–17

Consider:

Shield of faith. The Roman soldiers carried large shields made of wood. When an enemy shot flaming arrows, the big wooden shield would catch them and the flame would be put out. In battle, the soldiers would form a line with shields touching, so that the spears of the enemy could not penetrate. Consider how that relates to collective faith repelling the enemy.

The soldier of God catches those "flaming" lies that the enemy sends and puts them out. He has faith. Hebrews 11:1 defines faith this way: "To have faith is to be sure of the things we hope for, to be certain of the things we cannot see."

So when the enemy comes at us with a lie, we are sure of what God has said even if we can't understand it or see it. We operate on faith every time we turn on a light switch. We have faith that the power will be there.

Shields can be made of cardboard. The children can decorate them as they wish. They will need straps to hold them to the children's arms.

Helmet of salvation. The Roman soldier wore a helmet on his head. This protected his head from the weapons of the enemy. Salvation can protect our minds from the "knowledge" the world has to offer.

New words to learn or review:

1. Truth is sincerity and honesty; agreement with the facts; accuracy.
2. Righteousness: Right, honorable, just.
3. Salvation: The Hebrew and Greek words imply the ideas of deliverance, safety, preservation, healing, and soundness.

There are three tenses to salvation:

1. The believer has been saved from the guilt and penalty of sin (Luke 7:50; 1 Corinthians 1:18; 2 Corinthians 1:18, 2:15; Ephesians 2:5, 8; and 2 Timothy.1:9).
2. The believer is being saved from the habit and dominion of sin (Romans 6:14; Philippians 1:19, 2:12, 13; 2 Thessalonians 2:13; Romans 8:2).
3. The believer is to be saved in the sense of entire conformity to Christ (Romans 13:11; Hebrews 10:36; 1 Peter 1:5; 1 John 3:2).

Something to Make or Do:

Helmets can be made from plastic gallon milk jugs covered with aluminum foil or spray-painted silver; they're cute.

Armor of God (sword of the Spirit and prayer)

In this lesson, we come to the offensive weapons: The sword of the Spirit, which is the Word of God. Paul then adds, "And pray in the Spirit on all occasions with all kinds of prayers and requests." Ephesians 6:18

Scripture: Ephesians 6:10–18. A soldier who learned to love God: The Philippian jailer might have been a soldier. His story is in Acts 16:16–40.

Memory Verse: "And pray in the Spirit on all occasions with all kinds of prayers and requests. With this in mind, be alert and always keep on praying for all the saints." Ephesians 6:18 (NIV)

Consider:

1. The Sword of the Spirit, which is the Word of God.

    For the Word of God is living and active. Sharper than any double-edged sword, it penetrates even to dividing soul and spirit, joints and marrow; it judges the thoughts and attitudes of the heart.
    —Hebrews 4:12, NIV

    All Scripture is God-breathed and is useful for teaching, rebuking, correcting and training in righteousness, so that the servant of God may be thoroughly equipped for every good work.
    —2 Timothy 3:16–17, NIV

    The Roman soldier carried a short, sharp sword in a scabbard slung from a strap around his shoulder. This was only one of his offensive weapons, but it was one he could easily carry with him at all times.

    We can carry our swords, too, in our minds and hearts – that's why we memorize Bible verses and sing Scripture songs.

I have hidden your word in my heart that I might not sin against you.
—Psalm 119:11, NIV

Blessed is the man who does not walk in the counsel of the wicked or stand in the way of sinners or sit in the seat of mockers. But his delight is in the law of the Lord, and on his law he meditates day and night. He is like a tree planted by streams of water, which yields its fruit in season and whose leaf does not wither. Whatever he does prospers.
—Psalm 1:1–3, NIV

2. Prayer. Remember, we learned in the first verses of the section that we are not fighting *people* (flesh and blood), but unseen powers. When we pray, we do battle in the unseen, but very real, world. We cannot simultaneously fear and praise. And if, in the name of Jesus, we tell an evil spirit to depart, it must.

New words to learn and review:

1. Truth is sincerity and honesty; agreement with the facts; accuracy.
2. Righteousness: Right, honorable, just.
3. Salvation: The Hebrew and Greek words imply the ideas of deliverance, safety, preservation, healing, and soundness.

Something to Make or Do:

1. Swords can be made from cardboard and aluminum foil or silver paint. If possible, plan to have the children put on their armor and recite the Scripture for parents and friends.

Lesson 5–9

Bible Heroes

Overview: Children need someone to look up to. In our era, the people with the most "press" are often those we do *not* want our children to emulate. This series of five lessons will highlight several heroes of faith:

1. Joshua (who followed God's directions),
2. Esther (a queen for a moment in history),
3. Shadrach, Meshach, and Abednego (who followed God's law and refused to worship an idol),
4. Daniel (who would rather obey God than follow the king's edict), and
5. Jonah (who learned obedience in the belly of a fish).

These people obeyed God (or learned to do so), and so they are people our children can look up to. They can see that obedience to God is best.

Memory Verse: "Know, therefore, that the Lord your God is God; he is the faithful God, keeping his covenant of love to a thousand generations of those who love him and keep his commands." Deuteronomy 7:9 (NIV)

Joshua Follows Directions

Scripture: Joshua 5:13–15 – 6:27

Memory Verse: "Know, therefore, that the Lord your God is God; he is the faithful God, keeping his covenant of love to a thousand generations of those who love him and keep his commands." Deuteronomy 7:9 (NIV)

Consider: You are an army general, and you have been given orders to "take the city." However, you are not to attack or lay siege. You are to walk quietly once around the city for six days. On the seventh day, you are to get the army moving earlier because you will walk quietly around the city seven times! Then you are to shout, and the walls will fall down. Sounds funny to a general! But Joshua had had years of experience with the Lord's ways. He was one of the twelve original spies forty years earlier; he and Caleb had been ready to take the land then.

He followed directions and Jericho was taken just as God had said.

Our Children: This is a great story full of action and miracles. And it shows how God gets the glory for a great battle when the general follows directions and obeys!

Often, God asks us to do "silly" things in order to show His glory. This seems to be one of them. But Joshua did not argue with God. He did what God said to do!

Our emphasis needs to be that of obedience! We hide God's Word in our hearts, we know what He commands, we know what He requires of us, we listen for His voice, and we obey. The heroes we'll be learning about were ordinary men and women who obeyed and who were honored of God for that obedience.

New words to learn and review:

1. Obey – to carry out instructions or orders; to do what you are asked, requested, or commanded to do.
2. Covenant – a binding, solemn agreement

Something to Make or Do:

1. Act out the story
2. Veggie Tales: *Josh and the Big Wall*

Esther the Queen

Scripture: The book of Esther

Memory Verse: "Know, therefore, that the Lord your God is God; he is the faithful God, keeping his covenant of love to a thousand generations of those who love him and keep his commands." Deuteronomy 7:9 (NIV)

Consider: The book of Esther never mentions the name of God, yet God's presence is felt throughout. Esther obeys God through obedience to the man who raised her. When she was asked to go before the king to plead for her people, she knew what to do: fast and pray and get the strength of others with her.

Esther is a model of obedience. She obeyed her adoptive father. She obeyed the law of the land even at the expense of her freedom (harems were not noted for personal freedom of the women). She obeyed the king, her husband. And God honored that obedience by giving her an honored position – one that would ultimately save His people.

Our Children: This is a very complex story, and you probably will not read the whole biblical account. You could emphasize:

1. The beauty contest the king held to find a new queen
2. The year of beauty treatments and her favor with the man who was in charge of the harem
3. Esther is chosen as queen
4. The plot to kill the Jews
5. Mordecai's entreaty to Esther to go to the king
6. Esther's prayer and fasting
7. The banquet and the uncovering of the plot
8. The institution of Purim – still celebrated by Jews today

New words to learn and review:

1. Obey – to carry out instructions or orders – to do what you are asked, requested, or commanded to do
2. Covenant – a binding, solemn agreement

Something to Make or Do:

1. Act out the part of the story where Esther goes to the king.

Shadrach, Meshach, and Abednego in the Fiery Furnace

Scripture: Daniel 3

Memory Verse: "Know, therefore, that the Lord your God is God; he is the faithful God, keeping his covenant of love to a thousand generations of those who love him and keep his commands." Deuteronomy 7:9 (NIV)

Consider:

1. Why did Nebuchadnezzar insist that everyone worship the image of gold?

    a. he wanted to control them
    b. he was a man of conviction
    c. he was insecure
    d. he wanted to unite his people

2. How would you describe Nebuchadnezzar's officials?

    a. yes-men
    b. politically astute
    c. fearful
    d. alive
    e. loved the king

3. How could Shadrach, Meshach, and Abednego be so bold?

    a. they were crazy
    b. they knew what God had done for others
    c. God had saved them before

    d. they felt it was better to die than worship idols
    e. they knew the promise of heaven

4. Who or what was the fourth figure in the furnace?

    a. a son of the gods (as per Nebuchadnezzar, who, as a pagan king affirms "polytheism" or many gods)
    b. an angel (as per Jewish tradition – Psalm 91:9–12)
    c. Jesus Christ (according to ancient Christian tradition)
    d. an optical illusion

Our Children: This is another exciting story of God's rescuing those who are obedient to Him.

New words to learn:

1. Idol: an image of a god – in this story, the image was a huge statue
2. Obey – to carry out instructions or orders – to do what you are asked, requested, or commanded to do.
3. Covenant – a binding, solemn agreement

Something to Make or Do:

1. Sing the old Sunday school song "Three good men lived very long ago …" An online search will locate the words and music.
2. Act out the story.

Daniel in the Lions' Den

Scripture: Daniel 6

Memory Verse: "Know, therefore, that the Lord your God is God; he is the faithful God, keeping his covenant of love to a thousand generations of those who love him and keep his commands." Deuteronomy 7:9 (NIV)

Consider:

If I were being tried for being a Christian, would there be enough evidence to declare me:

    a. not guilty
    b. guilty in the second degree
    c. guilty in the first degree
    d. deserving of capital punishment

Besides jealousy, what might cause people to be interested in the private lives of public figures, especially "incorruptible" ones? Does having strong principles and values cause you to be more vulnerable to others, or less? Why? Our children probably already know this story. Our job will be to bring out parts of this narrative they might have missed before and to show again how God honors obedience.

New words to learn:

1. Idol: an image of a god – in this story, the image was a huge statue
2. Obey – to carry out instructions or orders – to do what you are asked, requested, or commanded to do.
3. Covenant – a binding, solemn agreement

Something to Make or Do:

1. Play a version of Duck, Duck, Goose that goes Daniel, Daniel, Lion.

Jonah Learns to Obey

Scripture: Jonah 1–3

Memory Verse: "Know, therefore, that the Lord your God is God; he is the faithful God, keeping his covenant of love to a thousand generations of those who love him and keep his commands." Deuteronomy 7:9 (NIV)

Consider: Jonah is different from other visionary books in the Bible as it tells of one incident in the life of the prophet. The Jews accept Jonah as an actual person (2 Kings 14:25), and Jesus referred to him in Matthew 12:38–41. Some, however, see this as a "fish story" which could not happen, and many get sidetracked by the fish. We tend to read this as a narrative, a story. However, it is located in the prophetic or visionary section of the Old Testament. Of course, God is able to do exactly and precisely what Jonah narrates. But many who are disinclined to believe the miraculous get preoccupied with the fish and miss the point of the book: God loved the people of Nineveh, too, and not only the Jews!

Our Children again will probably be familiar with this story. Show how this is more than an adventure; Jonah foolishly thought he could run away from God. God really wanted someone to show His love to the people of Nineveh (modern-day Iraq). Jonah finally obeyed, but he wasn't particularly happy at what God did. God chided him, though, and told the prophet that He, God, loved those people even if Jonah did not. God wanted some obedience from Jonah. It took three days and nights in a fish, but He got the obedience! Does God have to do that to us?

New words to learn:

1. Idol: an image of a god; in this story, the image was a huge statue
2. Obey – to carry out instructions or orders; to do what you are asked, requested, or commanded to do
3. Covenant – a binding, solemn agreement

Something to Make or Do:

1. Act out the story.

Lesson 10–13

The Fruit of the Spirit

Overview: When we ask Jesus into our hearts and lives, the Holy Spirit comes to live with us and to be the "earnest of our inheritance." When we learn obedience and surrender the sinful nature to the Spirit, He produces good fruit in our lives.

So I say, live by the Spirit, and you will not gratify the desires of the sinful nature. For the sinful nature desires what is contrary to the Spirit, and the Spirit what is contrary to the sinful nature. They are in conflict with each other, so that you do not do what you want. But if you are led by the Spirit, you are not under law. The acts of the sinful nature are obvious: sexual immorality, impurity and debauchery; idolatry and witchcraft; hatred, discord, jealousy, fits of rage, selfish ambition, dissensions, factions and envy; drunkenness, orgies, and the like. I warn you, as I did before, that those who live like this will not inherit the kingdom of God. But the fruit of the Spirit is love, joy, peace, patience, kindness, goodness, faithfulness, gentleness, and self-control. Against such things there is no law.

—Galatians 5:16–23, NIV

In ourselves, we will produce the fruit of the sinful nature. We might avoid immorality, drunkenness, orgies, and witchcraft, but that center section – hatred, discord, jealousy, fits of rage, selfish ambition, dissensions, factions, and envy – are produced by all of us from an early age! We need the Holy Spirit to produce His fruit in us. When Jesus lives within us, He produces it.

Let's help the children understand how Jesus/Holy Spirit produces the fruit of the Spirit, and let's show them how Bible-people showed those qualities.

The Fruit of the Spirit

Scripture: Galatians 5:22–23

Memory Verse: Galatians 5:22–23 "But the fruit of the Spirit is love, joy, peace, patience, kindness, goodness, faithfulness, gentleness, and self-control. Against such things there is no law." (NIV)

Consider: "Against such things there is no law."

Love: A deep and tender feeling of affection for or attachment or devotion to a person or persons. Wanting and desiring and working toward the very best for another person.

Joy: A very glad feeling. More than happiness, joy implies contentment, also.

Peace: Freedom from disagreement or quarrels; harmony. An undisturbed state of mind; serenity. Calm and quiet. When the Bible speaks of the peace that passes understanding, it refers to the calm, quiet spirit we can exhibit even during war or disagreements.

Patience: The will or ability to wait or endure without complaint: Steadiness, endurance, or perseverance in the performance of a task. Patience implies the bearing of suffering, provocation, delay, tediousness, etc. with calmness and self-control.

Kindness: Sympathetic, friendly, gentle, tender-hearted, generous. Kind implies the possession of sympathetic qualities, either habitually or specifically.

Goodness: The state or qualities of being good; specifically a) virtue, excellence b) kindness; generosity; benevolence. Good – Excellent of its kind. Honorable; worthy, respectable. Morally sound or excellent – honest, just, loyal.

Faithfulness: Showing the characteristics of a faithful person. Constant, loyal; showing a strong sense of duty or responsibility; reliable; exact; full of faith.

Gentleness: Having these qualities: refinement, courtesy, nobleness, chivalry, generosity, kindness, serenity; patience; not violent, harsh, or rough.

Self-control: Being in command of one's self or one's own emotions, desires, actions, etc.

We can always exhibit these characteristics. No laws prohibit us from showing kindness and patience. No laws prohibit us from being joyful. Which of these fruit are in the bud stage with us? Which are "on the vine" and mature? Let's show the fruit of the Spirit.

Our Children can understand and respond to these fruit just as we can. They can also learn to exhibit them as they become obedient to the Holy Spirit. These verses can be set to music in a catchy little song that the children will easily learn.

New words to learn: Actually all of the above. But for this lesson, let's work on the general concept of "fruit" and the concept that God produces the fruit in us.

Something to Make or Do:

1. Draw different "fruit" and give each a name: love, joy, peace, etc.

The Fruit of the Spirit – Love

Scripture/story: 1 Samuel 20 – The Story of David and Jonathan.

Memory Verse: Galatians 5:22–23 "But the fruit of the Spirit is love, joy, peace, patience, kindness, goodness, faithfulness, gentleness, and self-control. Against such things there is no law." (NIV)

Consider: According to the tradition of monarchies, Jonathan was to be the next king of Israel. Saul confided in him and said that Jonathan's kingdom would not be established "as long as the son of Jesse lives on this earth" (1 Samuel 20:31).

And yet, David and Jonathan were not rivals; they were fast friends! In this passage, we see how much Jonathan loved David, and we come to understand that Jonathan was giving up a kingdom to help his friend. Jonathan knew David had been chosen by God to be the next king in Israel, and the two make a covenant (ahhh, review word) that David would never "cut off his kindness from [Jonathan's] family" (1 Samuel 20:14–16).

Scripture tells us Jonathan loved David "as he loved himself" (1 Samuel 20:17). What a dilemma! You should be king next, but God has chosen someone else – your best friend! Can you love your friend enough to warn him that your father wants to kill him? Knowing that if your friend dies, you could be king? Jonathan was truly a man of God. Scripture doesn't say but if David was a man after God's own heart, could Jonathan be far behind?

Our Children might not know this story. Other curricula use the story of Jonathan giving David his coat. That had great significance in David and Jonathan's time, but I'm not sure our kids "get it." You can decide how heavily to explore the killing aspect. The Bible calls it what it is, and if we focus on the love aspect between David and Jonathan, we, too, can call it what it is without disturbing the children.

Words to learn and review:

1. Covenant – a binding, solemn agreement
2. Love – a deep and tender feeling of affection for or attachment or devotion to a person or persons. Wanting and desiring and working toward the very best for another person. Love is not selfish.

Something to Make or Do:

1. Make an "I love you" card for someone.

The Fruit of the Spirit – Kindness

Scripture: Acts 9:36ff – Dorcas – kindness

Memory Verse: Galatians 5:22–23 "But the fruit of the Spirit is love, joy, peace, patience, kindness, goodness, faithfulness, gentleness, and self-control. Against such things there is no law." (NIV)

Consider: Dorcas (Tabitha) was described as a "disciple": a learner, a follower of the way. During her lifetime, she "was always doing good and helping the poor." This woman was dearly loved; obviously her works of kindness came from her heart. She was a friend to the widows who came to show Peter the clothing Dorcas had made.

Joppa was and is a seaport town on the Mediterranean Sea. That likely means there were a lot of widows and orphans since many men probably lost their lives in the fishing or sea-faring trades. And Dorcas made garments for all of them.

After she died, Dorcas's body was washed and prepared for burial. Since they did not embalm bodies, and since the climate was warm, the dead were usually buried the same day they died, but burial might be delayed a couple of days.

Peter was called from Lydda, about twelve miles from Joppa. Peter was present at each of the three recorded times when Jesus raised people from the dead, so he certainly knew it was possible. As Peter prayed at Dorcas's bedside, he must have had a clear sense that God wanted this woman alive. Because of this miracle, "many believed in the Lord" (Acts 9:42).

Joppa was a Gentile, Jewish town, so it was common for people to have two names, one Hebrew or Aramaic and one Greek. Both Dorcas and Tabitha mean "gazelle" – a swift antelope. I wonder if Dorcas was given that name at birth or if it was a name given to her because she was quick to do things for others?

Our Children understand kindness. What can they do to show kindness to someone? Sharing toys or treats. Getting someone a drink of water. Helping put a bandage on a scratch. Giving a hug to someone who is sad. Picking up toys and clothes.

Even younger children can understand what it means to be kind. One of my favorite stories of my grandson, Sam, is this one: When Sam was about fourteen months old his mama dropped him off at day care. Another child had been dropped off, too, but this child was not happy and was crying. Sam went over to the child, offered her his Binkie, and patted her on the head!

Words to learn and review:

1. Kindness – when we are kind, we do nice things for people. We do the things they would like to have done, not necessarily the things *we* want.
2. Any others of the fruit of the Spirit.

Something to Make or Do:

1. Sewing cards. Use cereal boxes or heavy card stock and draw the outline of a child's tunic. Punch holes at intervals around the edge and use yarn or shoelaces to "sew" the garment.

The Fruit of the Spirit – Faithfulness

Scripture: Ruth – faithfulness

Memory Verse: "But the fruit of the Spirit is love, joy, peace, patience, kindness, goodness, faithfulness, gentleness, and self-control. Against such things there is no law." Galatians 5:22–23

Consider: Ruth is a great example of faithfulness.

Naomi and her husband had moved to Moab during a time of famine in Israel. During their time there, Elimelech (Naomi's husband) and her two sons died. That left Naomi and her two daughters-in-law. Custom at that time was that when a girl married, she married forever into her husband's family. Her whole duty was to that family, not her own birth family. Naomi decided to go back to her own country, and the two young women packed to go with her; it was expected.

We don't know why Naomi changed her mind as they were headed out of town that day. Maybe she remembered what it was like to be a woman in a strange country and had compassion on her sons' wives. Maybe in typical Eastern fashion she waited until the last to say the most important thing she had to say. But she released Orpah and Ruth from their duty to her, and she told them to go back to their own families. Orpah took her up on the offer, but Ruth decided to throw her lot with Naomi and the people of God.

Eventually, Ruth approached Boaz, the relative responsible for her and Naomi, and reminded him of that obligation. Boaz checked with the other near kinsman, and then he took Ruth as his wife.

Scripture tells us that the local women told Naomi that Ruth "loves you and has done more for you than seven sons," and to a Jewish woman, NOTHING was better than a son! Ruth was faithful to Naomi, a woman who called herself "bitter," and she was faithful to God. Boaz said that she showed great family loyalty (Ruth 3:10). The fruit of the Spirit was evident in her life.

Our Children live in a world where loyalty and faithfulness are not highly prized by the media. *People* value faithfulness, though, and we need to help our kids see how God blessed Ruth's faithfulness: she was honored in the community and in her extended family. God blessed her by giving her a husband and a son (who would become the grandfather of King David) and a place in the line of the Messiah.

Words to learn and review:

1. Faithfulness: Showing the characteristics of a faithful person. Constant, loyal; showing a strong sense of duty or responsibility; reliable; exact; full of faith.
2. Any other "fruit"

Something to Make or Do:

If you live in an area with crops such as wheat, barley, or other grain, obtain some "on the stalk" for the children to see and touch. If not, obtain some whole grain wheat, barley, oats, or other grain from a bulk food store so the children can see the grain in its "whole" state. If possible, cook some for a snack.

End Notes

I hope you have enjoyed flexing your imaginative muscles as you have helped the children in your care learn to hide God's Word in their hearts and learn the powerful stories that show how God's people adventure with Him.

The second year of BluePrint Lessons for Kids is in the works. See you again!

—Pam McLagan

Albany, Oregon

Are you responsible for teaching the Bible to children in your church or community?

Do you love children and want to encourage them to use the Bible as the blueprint for their lives?

BluePrint Bible Lessons for Kids can help. This blueprint is for parents, teachers, Bible club coordinators, and pre-school directors who want a framework for their own creativity. Lessons are grouped in three-month sections and center on a biblical theme. Each session focuses on a Bible passage and includes a memory section which links to several stories. Instruction can be tailored to different age groups or specific children in the group.

Kids learn in different ways. BluePrint Bible Lessons for Kids offers resources to use visual, auditory, kinesthetic, and tactile methods to target the learning styles of the children in their care. Kids can learn. People who love them can help!

Those who have used BluePrint Bible Lessons say

"The simple and short lessons give each of my teachers the opportunity to use any activities, crafts and teaching styles they are comfortable with. The timeline approach has been very effective in establishing a solid foundation for Bible truth in all our kids." –Tabitha Brinkley, Children's Ministry Coordinator, Abundant Life Center, Jefferson, Oregon.

"Each lesson focuses on the Word, providing a clear picture of the relationship between the Bible and knowing God. Children that have never seen a Bible eagerly recite the verses presented in each lesson. From creating the actual armor of God to acts of service to stories that speak to the children's daily lives, the BluePrint Lessons have it all." –Heather Gorman, Children's Ministry Leader, Jefferson Evangelical Church, Jefferson, Oregon.

Pam McLagan is a mom and grandmom who has been teaching something-or-other since she was fourteen. She's been teacher, education coordinator, and director of Vacation Bible Schools in the congregations she has been a part of. Professionally, she has taught in public and private high schools and is currently adjunct faculty in her community college's English department. Pam and her husband, Bill, have lived in Oregon, California, Indonesia, and Connecticut. They currently reside in Albany, Oregon.

Halo ●●●●
Publishing International

To order additional copies of this book call:
1-877-705-9647
or please visit our website at:
www.Halopublishing.com

www.ingramcontent.com/pod-product-compliance
Lightning Source LLC
Chambersburg PA
CBHW080537090426
42733CB00015B/2612